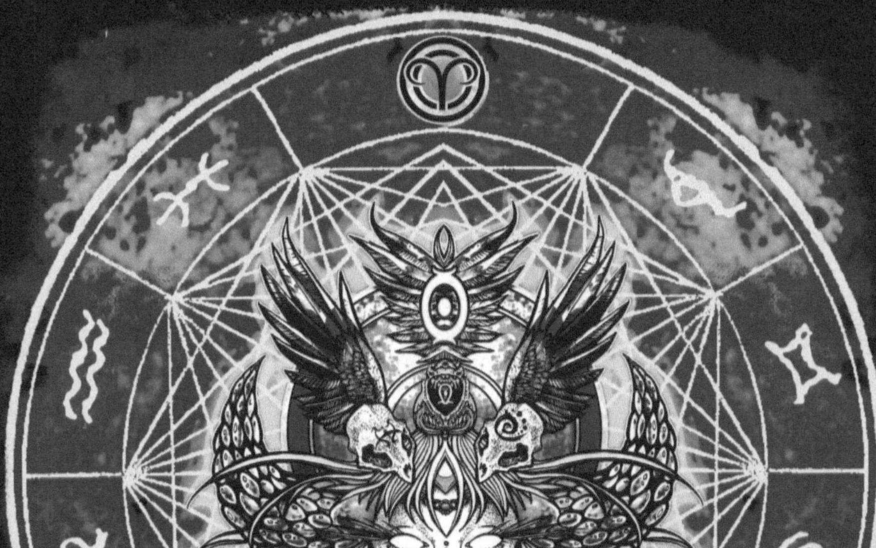

"In this book is contained the writings musings and artwork of the demented dimensional traversing subgenius of Tom Ambrose Denney to which who's portents are tried and true"- Cyphlon

The Living Void.

It is a dangerous thing to talk openly of the voices and visions which pour forth from the dark chasms of an unmastered mind. Existing inherently within the center of your brain is a portal into another dimension. This is the single eye of the majesty, our own unique imaginative vision which is of infinite vastness. It is divine. It is a direct connection to A living conscious void which acts as a gateway to all knowingness speaks in a language of symbol and omen. With meditation and discipline we find ourselves at precipice of this monstrous mouth of awareness awaiting to devour us we stand on a razors edge. The Uncanny Canyon where mystery and madness intersect. To master the vision of this while kept within the mind makes one an adept of that knowing so vast. The Adept is the walker between worlds on a tight rope of consciousness staring into the black oily depths of unknowing with one foot in the "real" world and one foot in this other realm of imaginative thought to which exists no ending. Here visions and voices emanate and dance freely through the dark waters of imagination where devils and angels battle for dominion.

The work is to bring those visions back from the kingdom of the Void unfettered by the monsters of shadow. Balance is the tool of this is peculiar realm where the visionary must dwell with trust that he shall not fall. It is a journey to perilous states of education through razors and angles. The initiated find themselves alone and accused of madness. The journey through the seven portals leading to the void is a solitary one, for the One is all there is and alone as One you must seek a unique passage back onto the golden comforts of creation.

Looking deeply into symbols and abstractions which pour forth from the void in mind is to peer beyond the veil into another sensibility entirely. Reflected in omens is the compass of the true Navigator. Easily can you stray, for there are many temptations in the shadowy subaqueous folds of the subconscious. The deeper the infinite, the more potential it has to consume you completely. These are dangerous worlds where One must tread with keenness like a sapient archeologist learned in the languages of the esoteric. This is to assist you in remembering your personal ascension access codes. Uncanny Canyon threatens to destroy the mind and soul of any too week to fight the tempest of bizarre emanations and mystical symbiosis as the transformation from being to Beingness undergoes that dark season of metamorphosis. Tread cautiously for within the oily chasms of the mind dwells the multi-tentacled Shadow, awaiting in coiled calculation to entrap the unsuspecting within a tempest of madness. The threat of eternal destruction is not unfounded. Many have lost everything to it's boundless hunger, a monster of sorts devouring the very deathlessness of a soul.

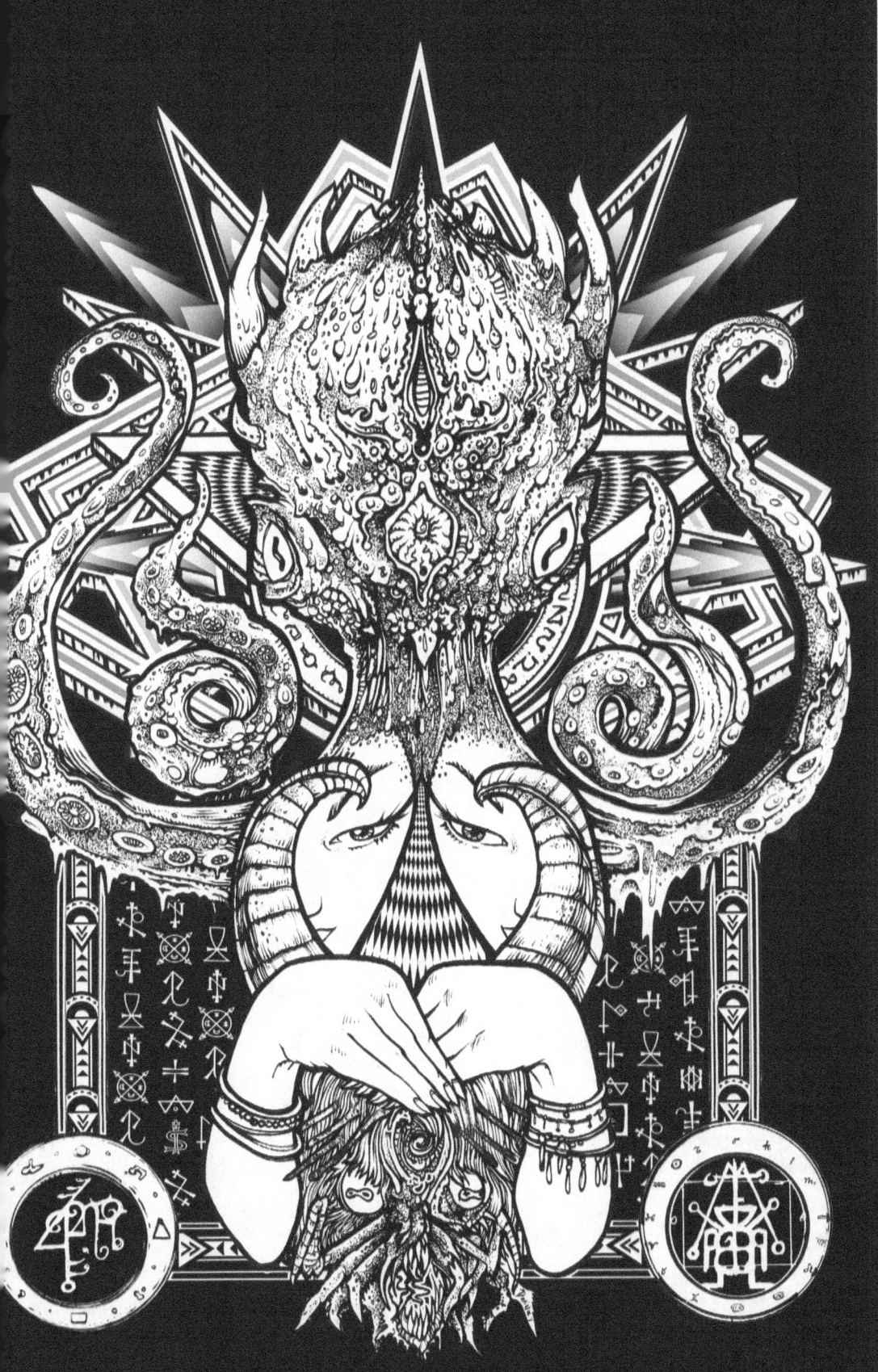

The Portal Dreamer

A Portal directly into the eye of chaos can only be managed by Mastered Mir
Through careful study of reality and consciousness does one awaken to this
ultimate liberation. Provided the keys of decoding, the Geometry, Symbolisn
and Intention are all in alignment. A trinity of
unfoldment reveals this astounding window into higher realms of thoughtful
awareness.

The door is locked and guarded and there are few who could even comprehei
its far reaching value even when presented with it. To the chosen few is this
work divinated as an aspect of silent reflection and unteachable knowing. To
find the keys to this portal and become its Master, one must be confronted
with the enigma of Spirit. It is through this force and this authority that awar
ness master shall unveil its multidimensional presence.

The unknowable aspect of a Hexagon is that it itself is the existing resonant
geometry of the field integral to portal technology. Walking the angles with tl
eyes is but one way the adept can achieve a discipline to unlocking the inner
eye without external stimuli. The lions share of the work is to come by this
awakening naturally. To speak of this to others is to invoke unnecessary resis
tance. The adept must keep the practice of this wisdom a solemn secret, and (
the pride in knowing this symbology must he swallow whole. For power told
power lost, and the key shall be pressed firm to the tongue in wardship. Hero
you will find the divergent path and in there the master key to mystic opera-
tions and alchemical initiation.

Initiation is an ignition, like a spark, like the opening of an eye to the dawning Sun. Practice in solitude the workings of the non material, those energies
at play on the opposite side of the veil. Play with the images of the mind and
make them become.

The triangle represent our world. Bridging the unfoldment from the imaginative realms of the hexagon in the tangible layers of the triangle is but one way
the symbols illustrate the momentum of thought turning into action. This
gateway we call a Vesica Piscis, that point where two circles bisect their coun-
terparts at their integer.

Peering often into this integer, that single point where your meditations meet
the Light of the mind is the sacred practice which all hierophant and master-
minds have kept. Since the ancient days of the great lodges of mystics which
existed on multiple dimensions were there torches of this early dawns light,
and passed was it to those who came to study at the temple. The temple exists
not in stone, but is in reference to the head where this portal of peering rests
in anxious anticipation of activation. The footsteps of the master walk silently.
In those silent waters will you open the portal. The principal of mentalism, po
larity, vibration and of agenda. These are the laws of the mental universe whic
shall be unlocked.

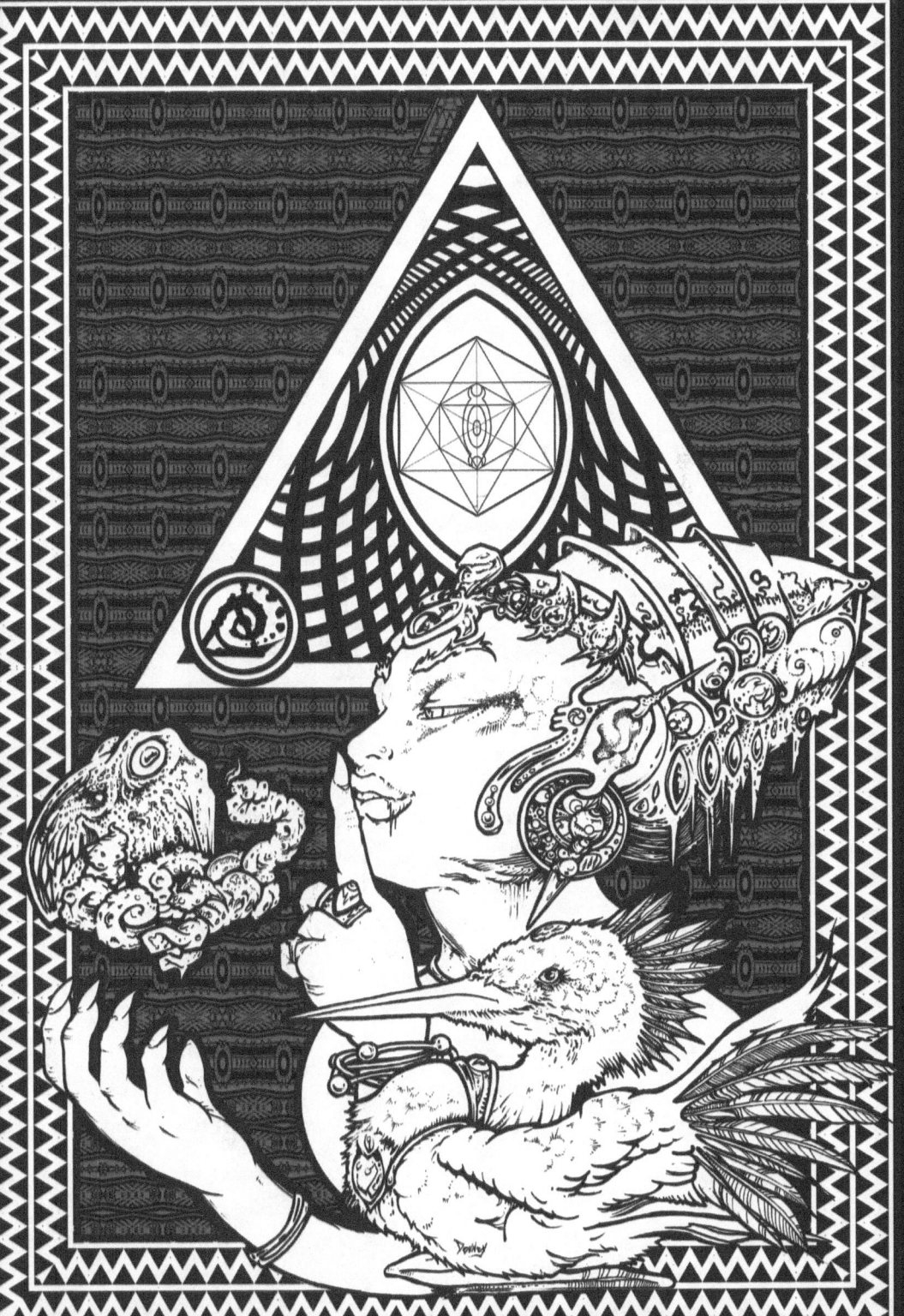

The Mask of Mystery

There is only one truth to the warrior of light should wish for, and that is to retain consciousness and pass through the spheres of death with aware-ness in tact. The legacy of this magical technology is not just a gateway to a higher realm, but a ladder for the consciousness to climb. The Key to unlock the dimensional veil comes from mindset, or a chosen lens of per-ception. Previously invisible and unimagined kingdoms of understanding and ability become clear once the proper lens of awareness is adopted. The twin serpents are the symbol of the discipline known as Kundalini. This is an aspect of the human body which doubles as a technology. The highest forms of technology would appear as magic to those not practiced of the master work. The alchemist is conversant with this intuitive technology on a steady basis. The wisdom of the portal shall be transmitted by activating and accelerating the electromagnetic resonance and harmonic proportions of the body which will feel like to electric snakes rising in tandem up the chakra system.

Breathing and mediation will raise the energies in the spine, activating the chemicals in glands and spawning shock waves of ecstatic pulsations. The serpents are a code for energy, creative force which must be awakened by action. Through the breath the melting of the ice encrusted glands fire up new thought paradigms. This is a birthright encoded within the DNA.

This is the awakening, the messages of mercury flow through this induc-tion of the turning the lead of mind into the emotional elixir of God. This is a sacred science of immortality. It is a knowledge based upon principles of evocation of the eternal divine.

Supernatural stirrings and old magic. This is to awaken and reconnect us to our High Priestess, our Higher Self, the seed of the great Creator. Our innate divinity is not bound by logic, or language. It is a cooperative inter-working.

The most terrifying element to the universe is the idea of eternal death. Consciousness can fragment, it returns to all. Ashes to ashes dust to dust, is a reference to a soul lost in the fall. Without careful study of self awareness, the soul will continue a spiral of reincarnation until the quantum source burns out. Replaying the same dramas without learning anything until the consciousness can no longer hold together and fragments back into the star dust. This is something every one does, but the adept who is self aware can do so in full consciousness, in full sovereignty, with full will power, Adashi Kryst star return. The fire of the mind is the same flame alight in every star. And when you combine with your light you shall live forever. To journey infinity at your behest rather than by the will of the rest.

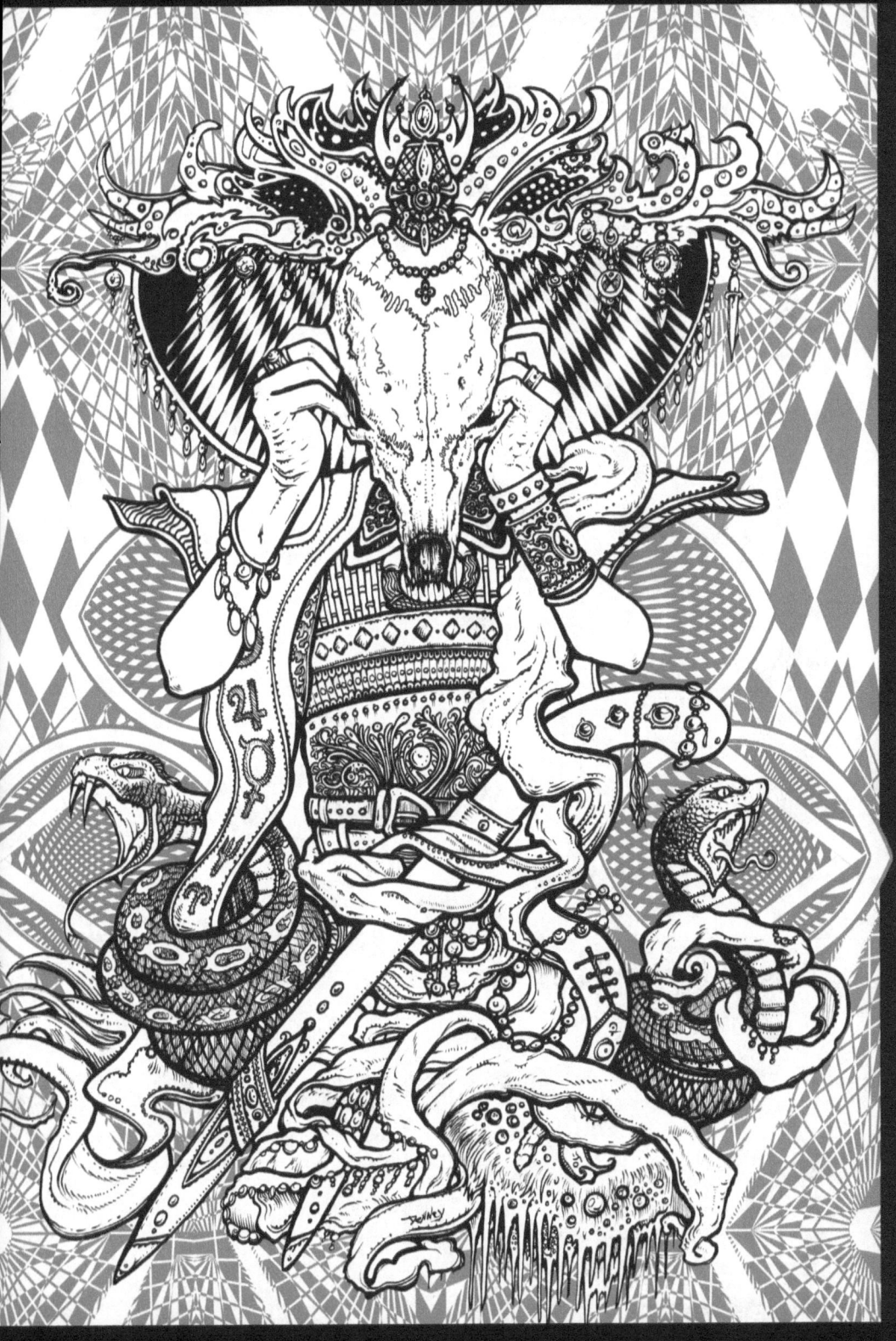

The Tree of the Sephiroth.

Indeed a strange namesake from an ancient time, that being the symbols and sounds we have inherited from our ancestors. Their names have been handed to us like a torch over dark canyons of epochs through vast expanses of mankind's entanglements with ignorance and ineptitude. They exist as spheres of influence illuminating the path of consciousness on its journey through the twisting labyrinth of form from origin to oracle. There in lies the mapping to the void of mind. Translated through many languages are their names with meanings past through many cultures with secret handshakes, in hidden lodges with veiled allegories only spoken in hushed tones under cloak and sword . Today, we shall for clarity simply refer to this map as The Tree of Life, and to its Sephiroth, we shall assign the term Sphere. Truth is the pillar of understanding by which the tides of time and Man has no power to tarnish. This voice is so familiar to the old soul, for it has likely taken this path from heaven to earth consciously before. Here is the key, and gazing upon its kriss crossed pathways and construction does the mind of man unfold . Bathed in ancient wisdom encoded by distant stars long extinguished is the mystic meaning behind each sphere and its association to solar alignments.

Each symbol is encoded with a profound science, which takes the key of intuition to unlock. Every aspect comes with a comprehension of its own magical technology. This is our most prized inheritance. Forefather gifted us such symbols for this time of our divine awakening, from deepest sleep in the lowest Dath do we ascend our own series of branches on the tree, our movements through the kingdoms. The evolving soul reads the high wisdom of every sphere. This is the energy manifesting through sine waves. The binary systems of the power of two, light and dark. A binary pulsation alluding to the physics of reality being similar to a computer program. The working schematics of the creative universe, and the life within it. The breath of life is in and out, the black and white is on and off. This is the heartbeat of timeless power. Such is the seat of wisdom. To put it simply, this is a spiritual map to understanding a hyper dimensional physics, the atlas of soul incarnation and experience in the physical third dimension. The lower kingdoms are wrought with reptilian shadows. These things child of light have I great wisdom in the overcoming. As you know light and shadow, thus you know the language of it. When you walk in light, you have power over all shadow, and as the torch of light stay ablaze in your heart and mind, so shall you know the method to overcome the throws of resistance on your path back to Creator mind. From Daath to Kether. Do you wish to be the programmer of your matrix coding?

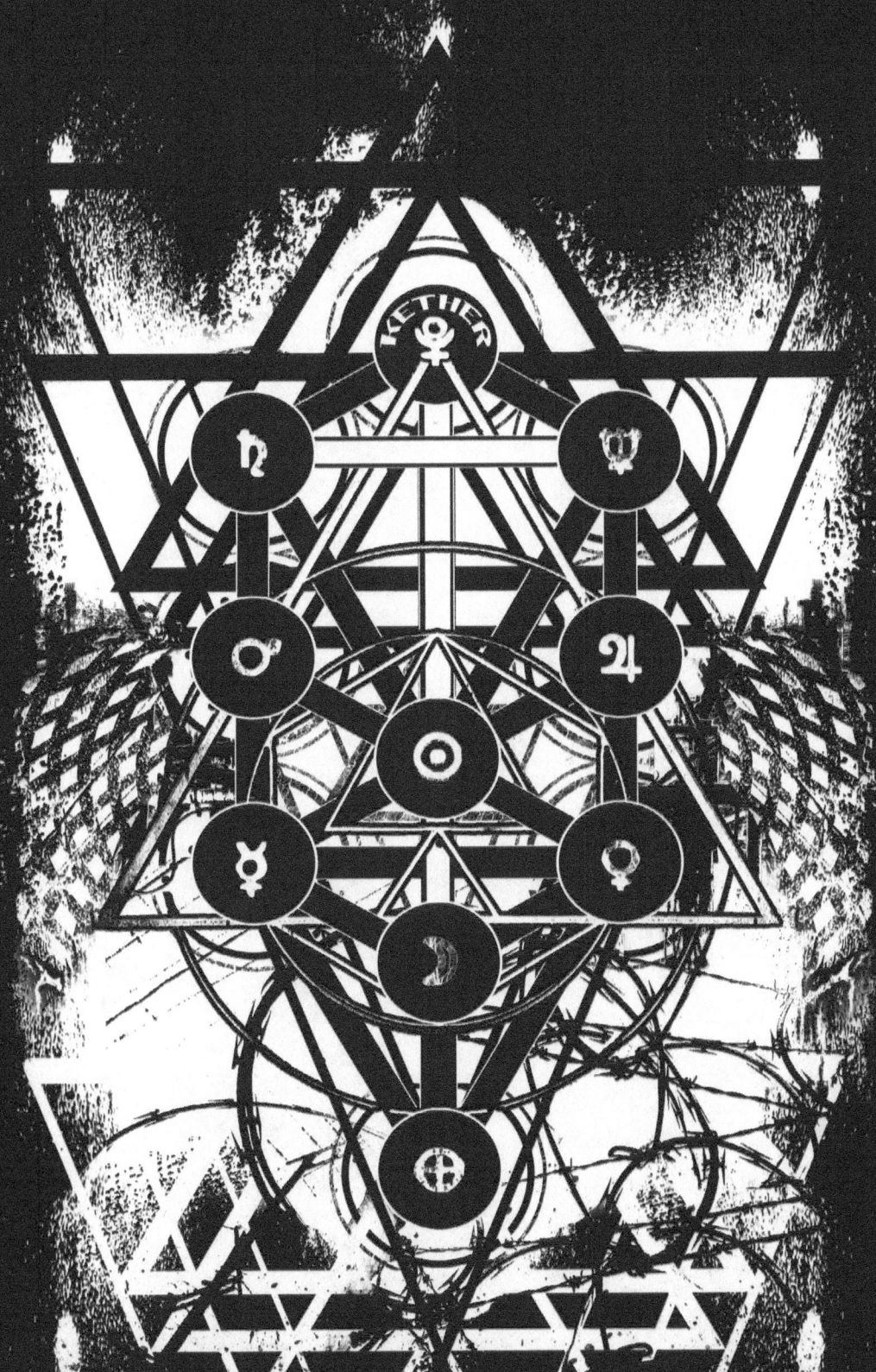

The Baphomet

For centuries Alchemists and Magicians have been drawn to the enigmatic and mystifying allure of the Baphometic physiognomy. There is something to it, some deeper mystery waiting to be uncovered. Every part of its symbology is layered in tripple meanings and subconscious refferences. Like a rubix cube, a road map for inner spiritual work to becoming greater than the lesser man.

A therionthrope, part beast, like the Pan but with the aspects of a winged-woman. It calls only to those who already harbor the scintilla of initiatory vision. Those with the will to fly shall find great influence here. A mixture of ambition and will to harness the vision and forge them into materium can be revolutionary. The Light is an imaginative sovereign, that free willed fire of mind. It harnesses that first fire of the One Creator who's embers lie dormant in all until the breath rekindle this flame overhead. The flame is the source of all things in potential. This is the rebellion against stagnation and the desire for change. The key to unlocking the limitlessness of imagination is to come upon the realm of the infinite, the eye that looks inward through flame. This is the realm where the sovereign dwells.

On the Tree of Life the Baphomet sits upon the Sephiroth called "GEBURAH". This word translates to English as "fear". Fear is a great burden, to which the lesser man be shackled by chains of shame and whipped by whimsy of corporeal desire. Just as Samson with his strength tore down the two pillars which bound him, so must we gather our own strength to overcome our fears, prejudice and judgement. This is a call to arms over even our more material trappings like addiction. For we are a slave to our vice. Through honesty and discipline only can we master the seductions of vice and liberate our selves from the slavery of covetous natures. For the result of lascivious infatuations is inevitable tears.

In the lap sits The Staff of Caduceus, the secret measure of the human energy vortex points. Where the Serpents cross is symbolic of the seven seals, or seven Chakras that are Sealed within and must be "activated". The serpents are raising out of the base, called "YESOD" or root Chakra, which is a Sanskrit term meaning "wheel of energy" or Vortex. This is KUNDAL-INI, or the Creative energy of the universe. We are to activate this series of vortex points and create a flow of energy from the Lower Natures to raise the fire in the Temple Crown. This seething breath of serpent energy is unencumbered by blockages of fear or the shackles of material desire. To engage the tantric breath is to truly feel this energy of connection move through the body system. and stimulating your pineal gland and liberating the thoughts beyond constraining belief programs.

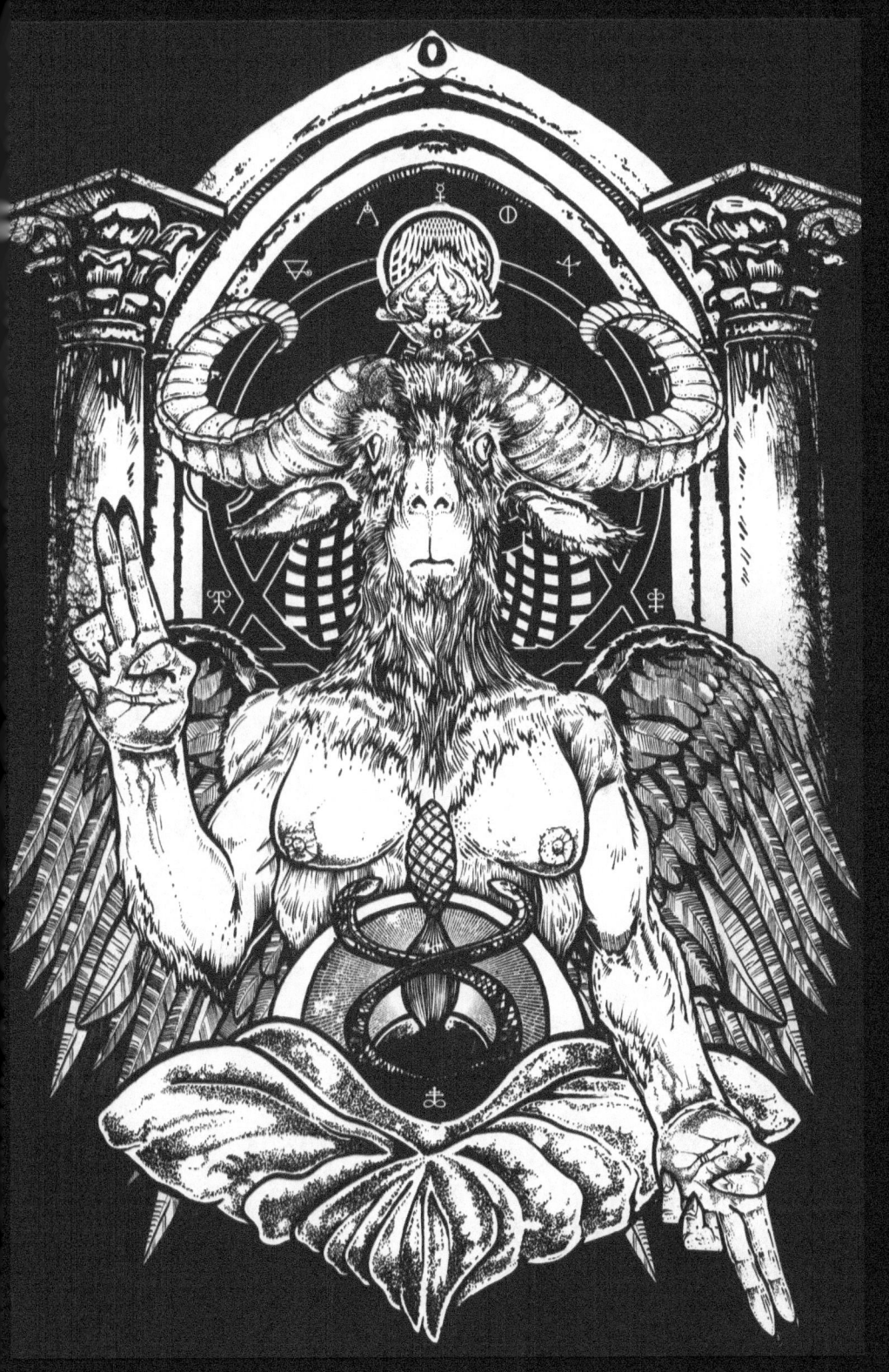

The Pinecone of the Pindar.

Creation injects influence upon the mechanizational workings of the multiverse. It is only the operator and the architect which may see the gears of time and illusion unfold as materiality. These workings are meant to stay hidden from the sleeper who fumbles through life with even a lower degree of existence than an animal, for their name is the sheep and the Magi be the shepherd.

Awareness with Inquisition; questioning everything in sight sets a light the torch of mind which bellows forth great fires of cosmic initiation. For within this is not just one Magi but an entire nation seated in the mind. I MAGI NATION. This flame reaches through time to illuminate the dark landscape of esoteric history, origin and future. The Trinity of multidimensionality on which the all is founded. This is the light of the inquisitive scientific spiritualist.

The mind which questions moves the hand that disrupts abominable paralysis and stagnation. Such a disruption is quite agitating to the muck and mire coated chasms which accumulate in its vast forgotten trenches the rotting pungency of moist writhing shadows nestled comfortably in pustulant unspoken vacums. They might call this light rebellion. For growth is beset with anarchy to the established coffers of unexercised stasis.

An apparatus of a decayed Roman empire with the holders of Solomon's Key at the center of the great building work. This is also when alchemy took root as the science and divination tool of the monarchy by way of their own spiritual adepts. Historical Alchemy existed as a style of Western Shamanism founded on Egyptian symbols and terms. The golden soul is raised from the impurities of material man and into the higher realms of becoming through this creative practice.

If there is devil, it exists only in the mind of man. When man does heed the voice of desire and allow its dark works to guide his hand, it is man and only man that be at folly for fulfilling the works of such evil on demand. This is the force of ignorance which keeps humanity chained in eternal bondage to the aspects of his material nature.

Though within grasp that imaginative power to mold reality the genetics of humanity are sprung from the soil of animal survivalism. This is a warning about using the power of source for the left hand path, in which case magical achievement are geared towards service to self above all other creation. Under such a path everything turns upside down, Helter Skelter. When the power of intent is focused on corporeal lust, envies, or selfishness the result is inevitably tears. The Fools journey is wrought with such perils so that a fertile and honest heart be his trusted compass towards becoming the enlightened and build a bridge to the Golden Angel.

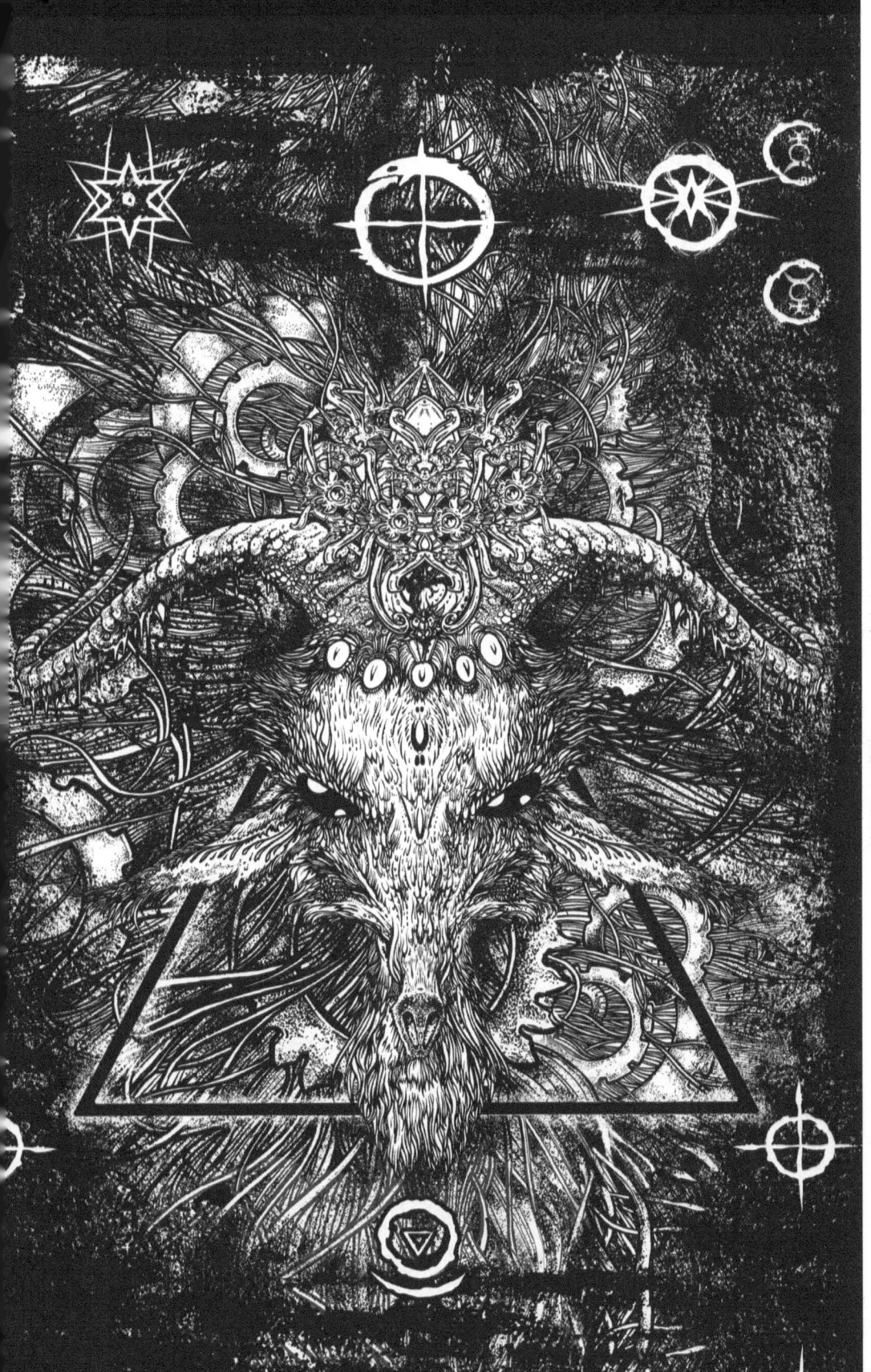

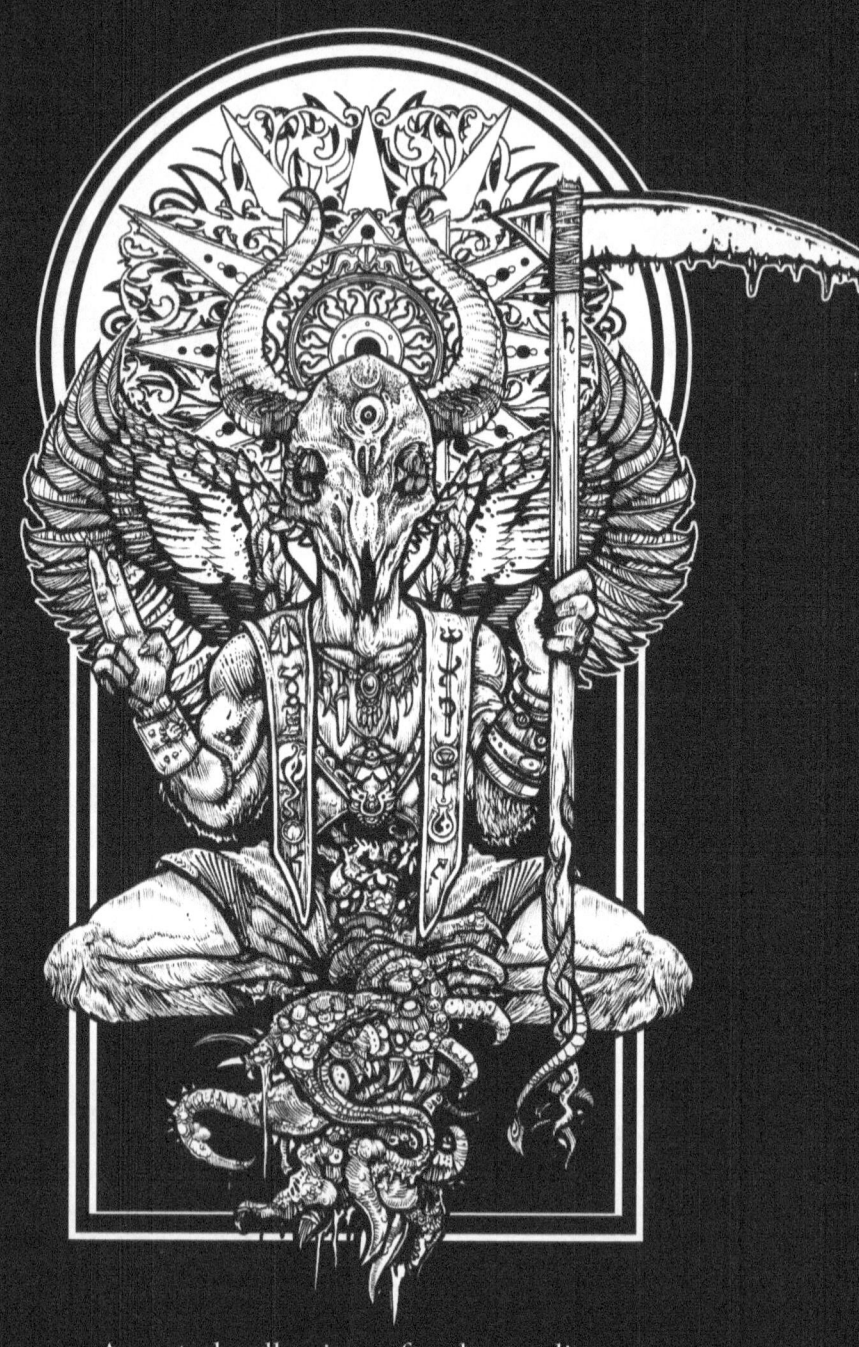

Ancestral wellsprings of understanding
through deep cellular knowing

SATURN

Oh mighty Lord of Times yours is the way of the law. Elder keeper of the days and night how far your reach is and how vast your sight. The cycle of dark unveiling begins with the sickle of Saturn. Saturn is the lord of chaos and destruction. He teaches you a lesson and he will take your very life if you fail to heed.

Looking deeper into this archetype of the cosmos should lift only the surface veil of this massive cornerstone of esotericism. Saturn was very important in the religions and cultures of the ancient world and is still today. His symbols and influence work beyond the lens of mundane perception. Saturn is an energy and an effect but is also on the most terrestrial level a planetoid engulfed by moons and shrouded in satellites. It is an alien world on a

different vibration of truth, a different law which reigns down upon our Earth in a magnetic trowel of elevated influence. By way of this influence occurs challenges, provided as divine testing. Saturn offers to our free will the option of the dark side, the Black Tantra. Though tantalizing on the surface the adept remembers that the sparkles are only the reflection of light, and not the living light itself. Fetid is his wisdom spoken from tainted throne aloft the Black Square. Kronos knows no limits and will provide a ceaseless bounty of illusion that lead inevitably to suffering. By this pendulum of temptation and empty fulfillment do we find the fire by which we shall burn away the impurities of our human beingness.

Be it Alla, YHWY, or Kronos or Ell, all names lead back to the square. It is a planet of the watchers, the fallen angels crowned by the cycle of the Elohim. Man is the measure of all things, and his sign is the pentagram. Yet YHWY is the law which imposes himself on the psyche of mankind, and the old path is that of the square within the hexagon. The old path is the mystery religions which hold a knowing about the extraordinary astral travel the consciousness is capable of. There is even an eternal hexagonal storm churning on the surface of the planet Saturn. It is a vast mystery who's contemplation brings lavish vision.

For all his power, Kronos is a fallen god who has severed himself from the quantum of creation, and has turned to vampire mechanics. The most important element of psychic defense is how to disengage from the tentacles of vampire entities which are feeding off of what is in simple terms, your eternal soul. In truth this whole system is a type of energy siphoning matrix which will in time, drain your spark of light the way a black hole consumes the energy of a sun. Through light shall you escape from this web of soul vortex consumption. Retain eternally your living spark.

The HIGH PRIESTESS

She is the manifestation of the subconscious. Behind her is the veiled mystery of that greater realm, that deep place of creative emanation.

Above is the higher consciousness, coming from a different dimension, one without limitation. We as acolytes of the sovereign are grounded within the third dimension. There she stands as the guardian between these esoteric realms. The keeper of the great secrets, and a knower of the sacred principles of nature, the balanced understanding of the workings of time and space and the key holder to the unfoldment of reality. It takes a magician to step to her temple and hear the subtleness by which she speaks her knowing upon the wind and through visionary dreams. Between the polarities of light and dark Between the Pillars of Jachin and Boaz

In between is where we find our intuition, our inner guidance. In between the breath is where we find her temple. In the silence of place in between the inhale and exhale. This is where you invite the light and absorb it into the body and into the heart. This temple is the vortex of the heart. When we initiate communication with this internal place we hear its wisdom the soft subtle tones of the most high. We exhale limitation, we breathe out encumbered belief systems. We release toxic noise, clamoring thoughts and the clutter of the mind to find her.

She is the quiet voice, underneath the layers of noise. Speaking all the time through the matters at hand, through the predicaments of life. Always the secrets are in plain site, but only if you have eyes to see and ears to hear. Like the owl that flies with silent wings in the pitch black, so too must we take silent stealth on our flight through those places where light is most absent. In its talons the Torah, reminding us of the teaching of Solomon "AS WITHIN, SO WITHOUT". For our intuition knows that the inner realm of the subconscious is that which creates and projects reality. To come onto the source is to walk a path to the heart, and breathe deep the light of the creator. So as you feel in the heart so shall you find in your world. There is the balance of the mind of nature and the mind of the infinite working in congress to create a symphony of harmonious existence. The world will only be a reflection of your attitudes towards it. For her, the two pillars are topped with the Sephiroth known as Binah and Chockman, which is Love and Creativity. By these subtleties shall the hand weave a most intune awakening and the weaving of a harmonious pattern of being. The "Occult" or "Hidden" truth is given through initiation. Only then are you granted passage beyond the veil of the Exoteric, or outer teaching, to the land of the Esoteric where greater wisdom is perceived. Such wisdom calls to us to return to a forgotten age of beauty and enlightenment.

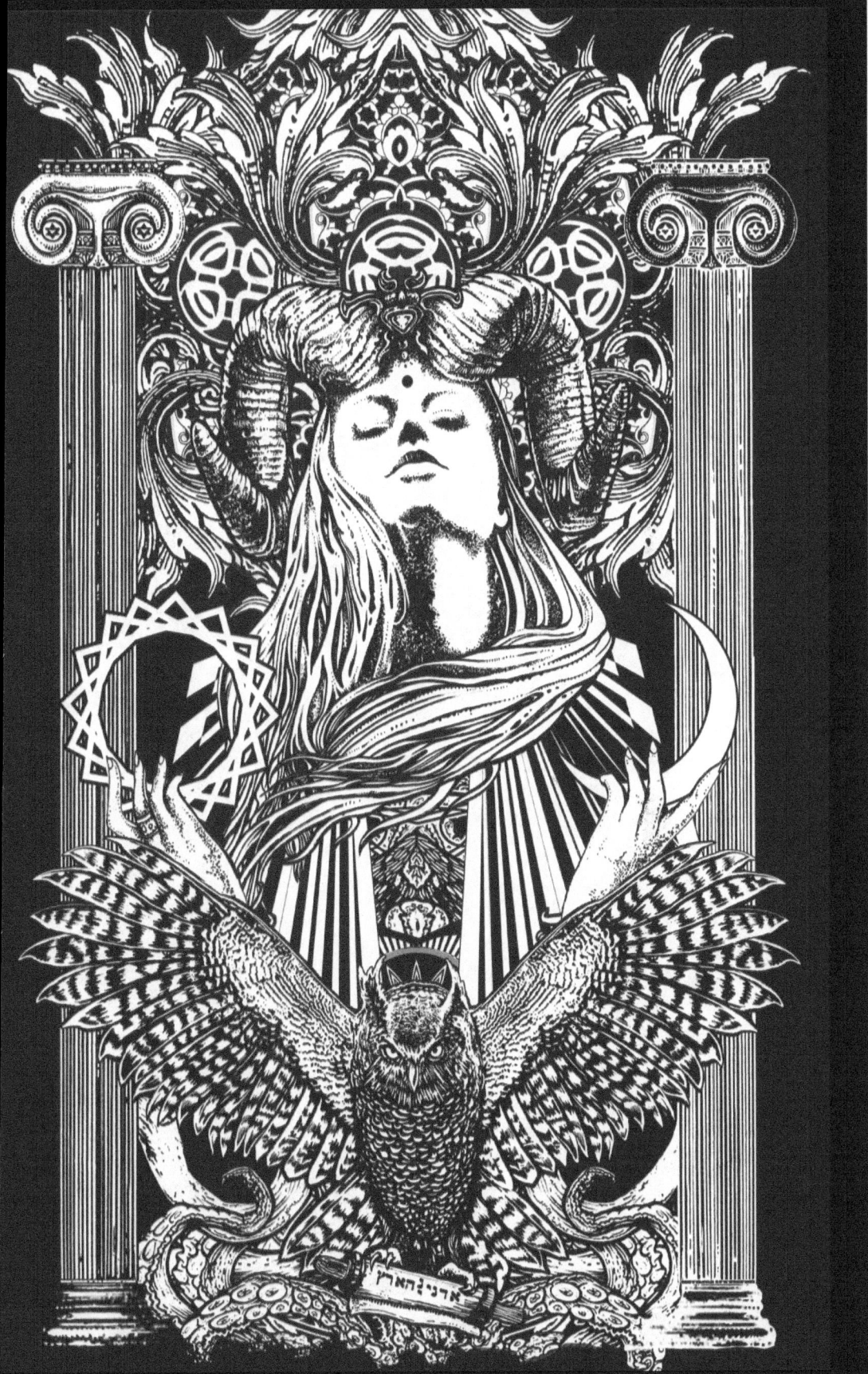

Communing with Spirit

Multifaceted are the aspects of the Spirit as too the Ibis. An entity with the ability to transcend dimensions, take flight from Earth to Heaven. It represents the communal arch connection, the messenger of the void.

Held Sacred in most ancient Egypt, the Ibis was associated with Thoth, the Lord of Truth and wisdom. In the aspects of the shape of the Ibis are inherent the spiral curves of the Fibonacci sequence, that organic unfoldment of nature concealed in the curve of its beak. Trimegistus, representing the Moon, Intuitive Magic and the inventor of Writing, riddles and the secret schools of ancestral reverence. In him lay the tools of life, the Emerald Meditator.

The Egyptians regarded the entire universe as an act of Magic, mainly the materialization of consciousness into physical form. As with most encoded esoteric artworks, this is a delineation of the mind .The secret is the pathway this consciousness should travel from corporeal form back to a divine source. Between the pillars stands the princess somewhere between life and death, between day and night, between the lines of black and white. The union of sun and moon, there is the dweller between two worlds, the Soul. Her's is the knowing of all things, as she treads the prefaces of that living void. Through the tears of suffering birthed from material desire comes comfort in the embrace of higher knowing. As we turn our gaze inward, so does the blossom of the mind reveal its beauty in wondrous unfoldment. This the touch of the divine will wash away the tears with understanding, embrace you within the folds of its creative awareness and assist you in transcending the mundane abstractions of fear and trepidation.

Through silence we find peace. Like the wind through the feathers of the thunderbirds, a message is carried. That voice of conjuration, reminding one that gifts of abundance are inherent. The Magi knows that if the Eye be single, the power of the living void awakens within and through such all things are possible. For as you think, and as you write, so shall it be. This is the power Thoth wishes to remind us of. So hold your tears Goddess, this is your creation. Weep not for the departed, shed not a tear for that pain, for such is the machinations of the untrained mind. Only with most careful introspection, decoding and exertion of intelligence can we awaken that boiling source of infinite majesty, our inner Sun.

Strengthen your focus as you enter the temple, for you are the privileged initiate. The secret teachings are your vehicle out of suffering and into a realm of advanced existence, with sight beyond sight. The reward of this pursuit is eternal life. This should occupy your heart for so is the way to the self. Let it be coveted, the act of communing with the god force internal.

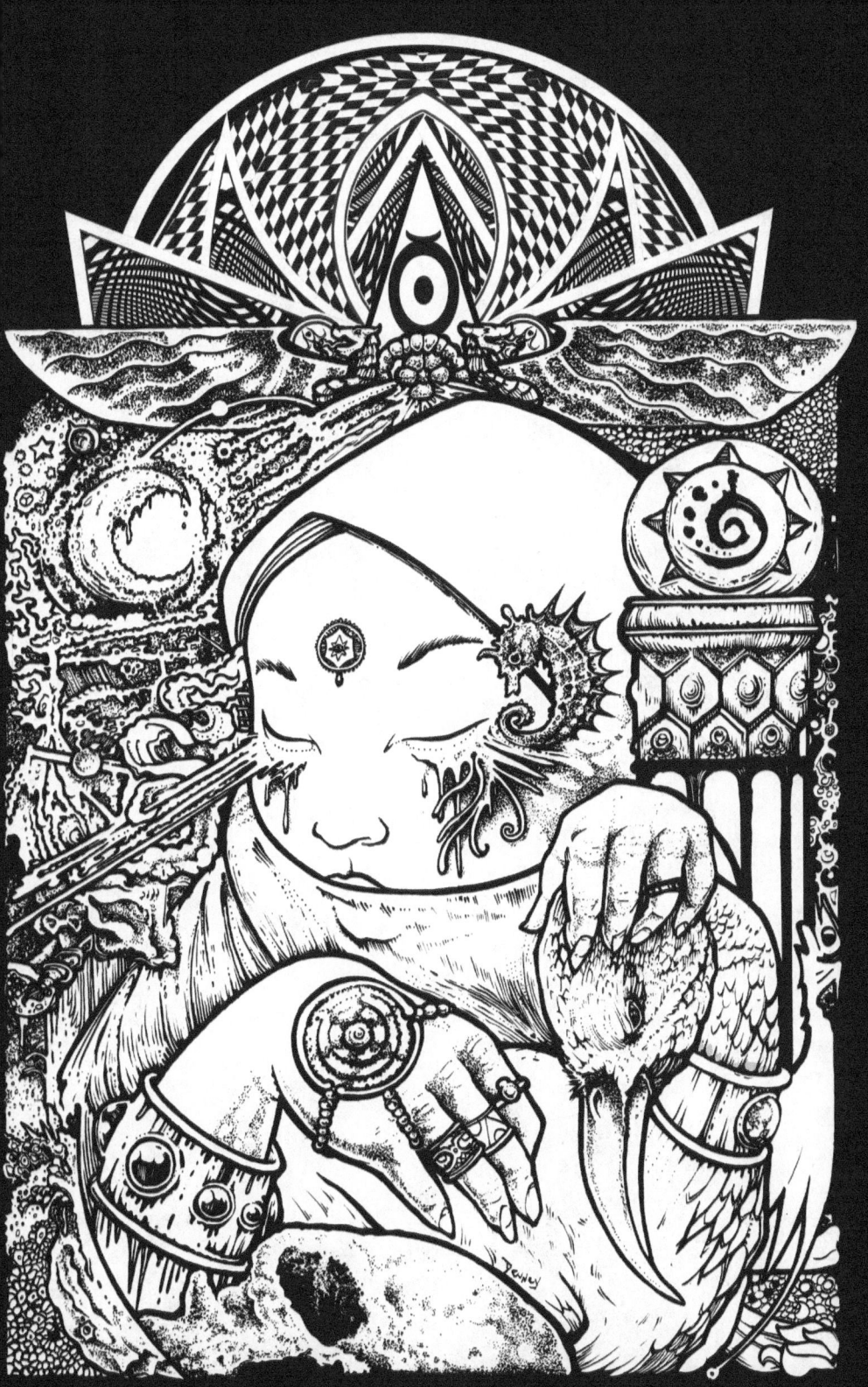

The Reptilian Shadow

The brighter the Light the greater the shadow cast.

In our journey through the Tree of Life, we must begin at the root of things. The slimy muck of old decay which nurtures and fertilizes new growth. Though we are spirit, our life body evolved from the dirt and it is our lower natures which we often find conflict in embracing and taming. As we ascend the tree we grow in our own consciousness moving ever towards the higher aspects of creation. How a tree does grow from the darkness of the soil, made up of rotting matter and old decay, to graze the sky reaching towards the sun with growth. So too it drinks the water of life and reconstitutes the nutrients of the old, the seed unfolds and ascends a sprout unfolding to new dimensions. The sky holds ever that burning source of life, the sun. So too we fertilize our journey from the mulch and muck of our base beingness into evolution.

DNA handed to us by our ancestors over vast epochs of time, the collected contagion of a million different life forms and incarnations remembered and unveiled in our modern physiology wrought with the desires of animalistic origin and crafted into Human Sapieace.

Again the serpent is a symbol of Unity becoming divided. It is a symbol of energy, the arts coming to creative faculty, vibration in sine wave of intensity. It creates an emotional response which has a trigger embedded and operated from deep within the subconscious. This is the initiation of the heart, what lies beneath. Something that can not be seen, only felt. It is the work what will adjust the vision to the invisible underlying causes, the templates of reality and a road map to operating in higher realms.

Yesod, the foundation. The reptilian animalistic foundation on which our human body was designed. Base desires of the shadow will deceive, for the all desire results in suffering. Fed by the sexual energies, Eve and Adam. The serpents are the two candle sticks standing before the god of earth. The call is to leave behind the reptilian perception and raise the consciousness to a higher plain of perception. This is the souls resurrection and the return of the child to the light of the creation. This will intern liberate hidden abilities.

By raising our kundalini and putting to fire the impurities of our corporeal aspects we transmute our base nature into gold. This journey of adept. These deeds of virtue redeem themselves etherically as great coffers of experience and wisdom. These are the golden fibers that grow along the crown of the mind awakening. The dawn which is gold is in accord with the heart of those who seek righteousness and the reward of the universe is abundance.

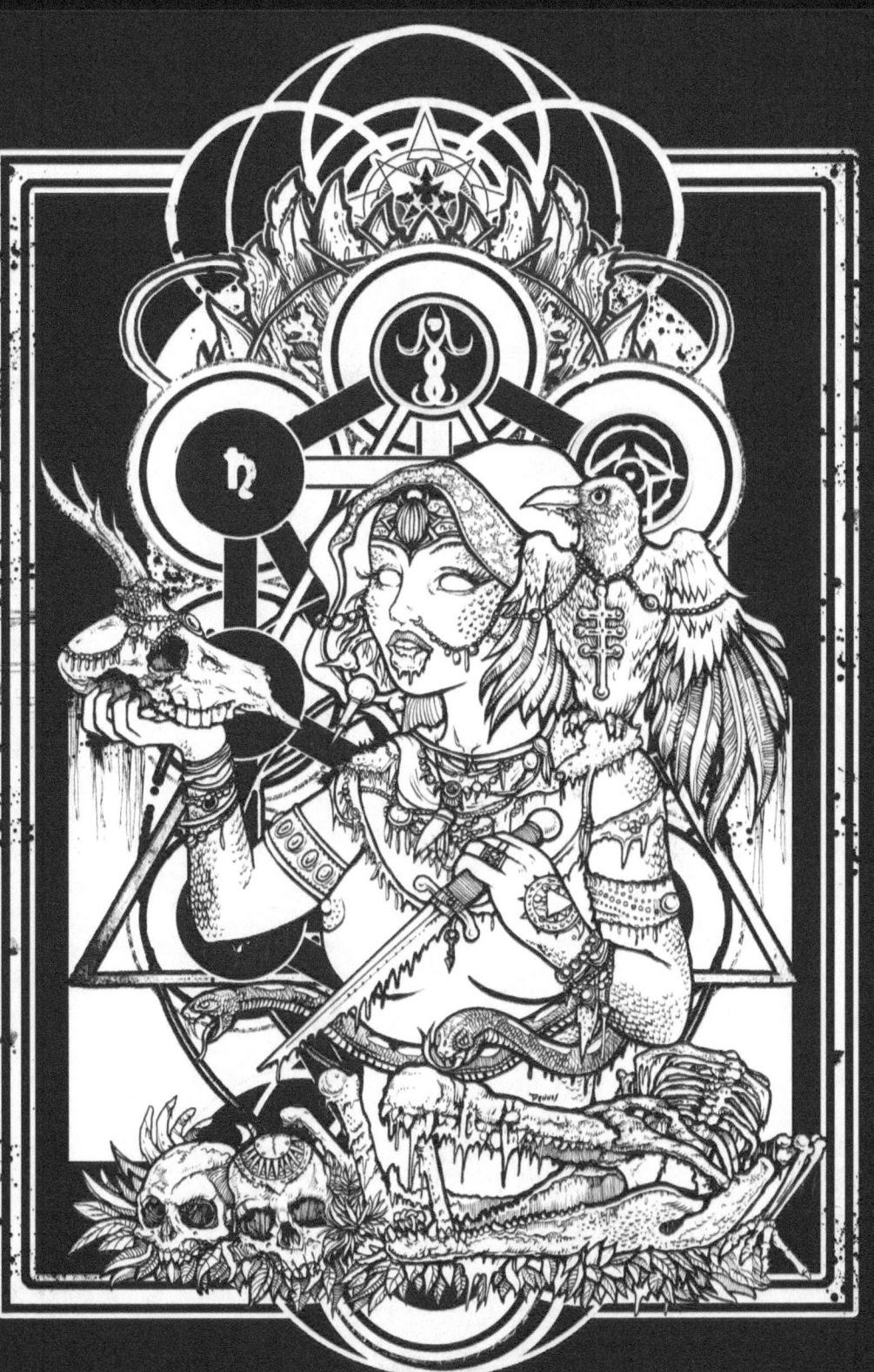

The Dragon of Resistance

When ever abundance is called upon, so too a call goes out to its polar opposite. It will appear as dragon to nest at the gate and block its flow while feasting at the shimmering pools of majesty. This fowl serpent of miscreance must be castigated and circumscribed by the noble seeker of immaculacy on sight. The sorcerer who dons such robes of purity as to delineate the sacred union with the maiden, the High Priestess of the mysteries, will inevitably find through such work that his life has become imbued with alchemical bits of gold. Where ever gold begins to accumulate, around the feet of the maiden, a dragon will inevitably be attracted like some strange magnetism. This is what we would describe as "resistance". In man the resistance is an aspect of the Ego which loathes change, innovation and in general work which strives for elemental purity and connection to highest self. It will with all its might interfere with the path and question, challenge, berate and endanger the seeker. It evokes the warriors call, the ignition of the sword within. Every noble knight must prove his worth over such force. Once mastered the sword of discipline will be the alchemists greatest ally in the quest for the attainment and keeping of the maiden's hand, the very portal to higher realms.

We are responsible to be the knights of the portal, the protector of our priestess. When a dragon takes onto this course a swift justice must be enacted in the form of discipline and focus. Such virtues will attain you subsequent riches ten times that of which you started. For resistance is a teacher in disguise, and the stronger it is, the greater will be avancement of the soul once resistance is conquered.

The mind is a war room where strategies of victory over the dragon must be conjured and implemented. The desire to coddle the self and indulge in passing pleasures must be put to the flame. For only fire can temper steel, and it is only the most stolen of steel wills that can cut the hide of the dragon and cleave its reptilian heart.

This is purely physics. All change flirts with the dragon, and always must this impediment to growth be vanquished like the fowl scaly sulfur ridden monstrosity that it is. There can be no compassion for weakness or no tendency towards leniency in the quest to whiten the robes of the auric field so that the light of creation can shine through every fiber and reveal the greatest treasure of all. That is the vast god like chauffeurs of the disciplined mind, doing the work that needs to be done each day while walking the treacherous path of mastery. One misplaced step can eternally dash the knight into the mouth of the serpent. It is a mouth of madness which awaits to consume those who folly. What is left of their mind will be devoured over a thousand cycles of endless black holes and destinationless voids acting as gateways to arenas of tumbling chaos which consumes itself repeatedly and eternal.

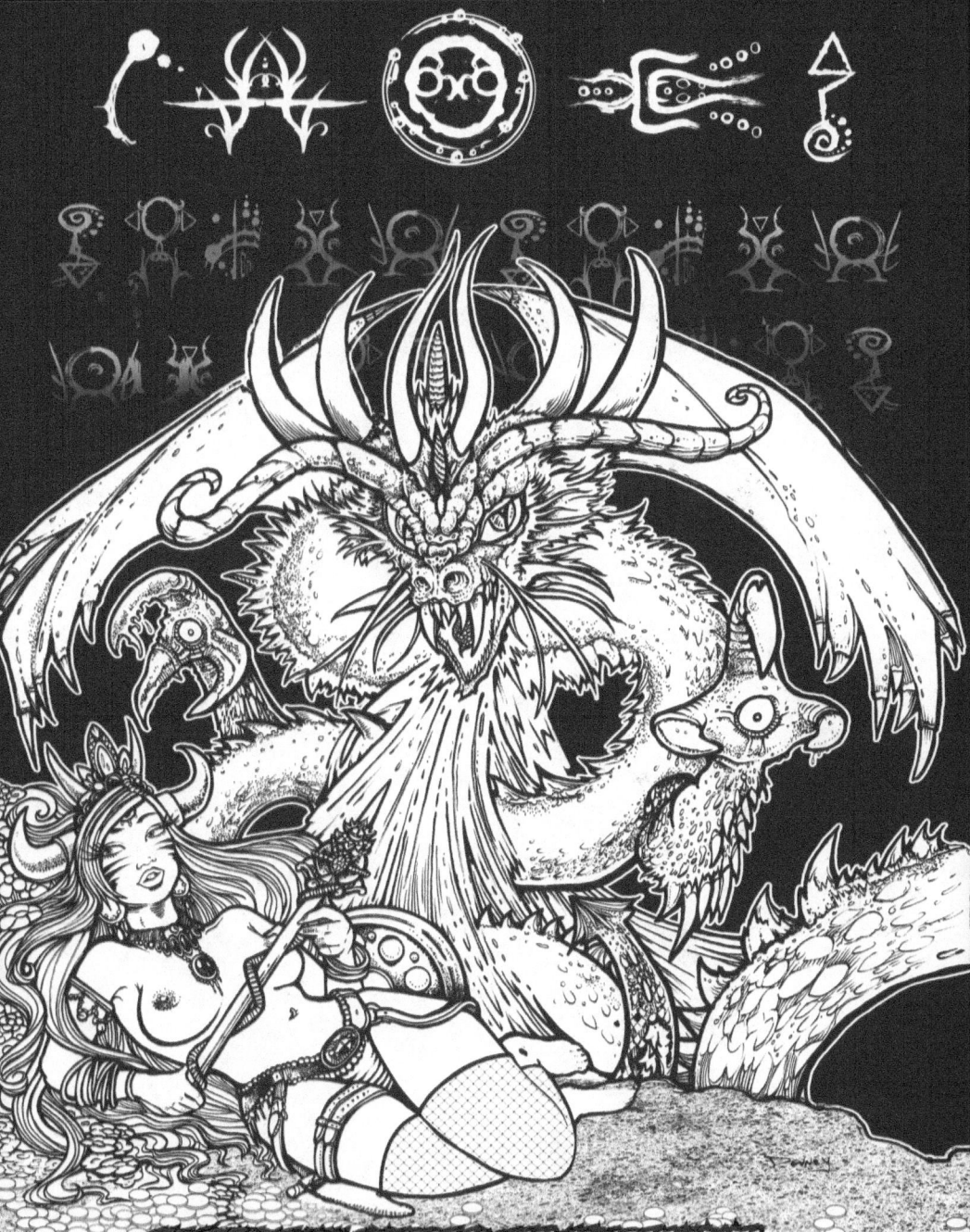

THE UNIVERSE WILL CONSPIRE TO MEET MANS DESTINY, YET THE MIND OF MAN IS BISET WITH CHALLENGES, DISTRACTION AND COURSE ADVESARIAL FORCE WHICH INHIBIT GIFT ACCEPTANCE, WITHOUT WHICH THIS LEARNING EXPERIENCE WOULD BE NAUGHT

What was Parasite

At the swamp you might find your self accompanied by blood sucking leeches and mosquitos, so too are there similar entities on the etheric realm. These creatures which parasitically feed from the energy emitted by negative emotions of humans and suffering of animals are disconnected from the source of life, so they must survive by siphoning it from unknowing hosts. Humans have a series of energy bodies which extend out from the physical much like the subtle layers of atmosphere which separate the Earth from the vacuum of space. These energy bodies can be perturbed or perforated so that life force seeps out from the individuals core and into the ether. The most common way of etheric soul seepage is due to negative emotions. When one feels sad, lonely, depressed, paranoid, jealous, heartbroken or any variety of fear, one will leek not only tears, but emotional energy. This appears as a puff of steady cloud type substance which has its own unique smell and taste in a fifth dimensional sense. Like blood attracting sharks in water from great distances, these creatures congregate and swarm on a person suffering sorrows or folly. They descend down to feed on the negative emotions, which is often why people describe feeling "heavy" or "burdened by the weight". They will describe a demon on the back or a monkey on the shoulders or in many cases will say "something came over me". This is the psychic knowing that one has become afflicted by way of these negative energy drinking parasites. The most terrifying aspect of these pesky entities is that they latch on in some cases growing tentacle like roots deep into the chakras of the host and seed the host more of the thought patterns which triggered the initial energy loss. It is a conscious effort on the part of the parasite to continue the patterns of negative emotions so that the delivery of their food will be insured. They prefer anything insidious, debaucherous, depraved and lecherous and most especially the prefer to feed on anything blasphemous in the light of creation. Such emotions seem to set about a feeding frenzy. Any acts against creation seem to give these entities even more delight as they become bloated from the guilt and consternation of the victim, effectively derailing the life course and subverting the very destiny of the victim. Alcohol and Tobacco are great examples of physical addictions which usually have their origins in the intentions of these parasitic beings. To the point where it is more comfortable for the host to indulge these vices even to his own detriments rather than to doing the work of weeding out these destructive influence from inside. These creatures operate outside of time lines, so they can effectively get into one lifetime, and move forward and backwards in lifetimes affecting subsequent incarnations.

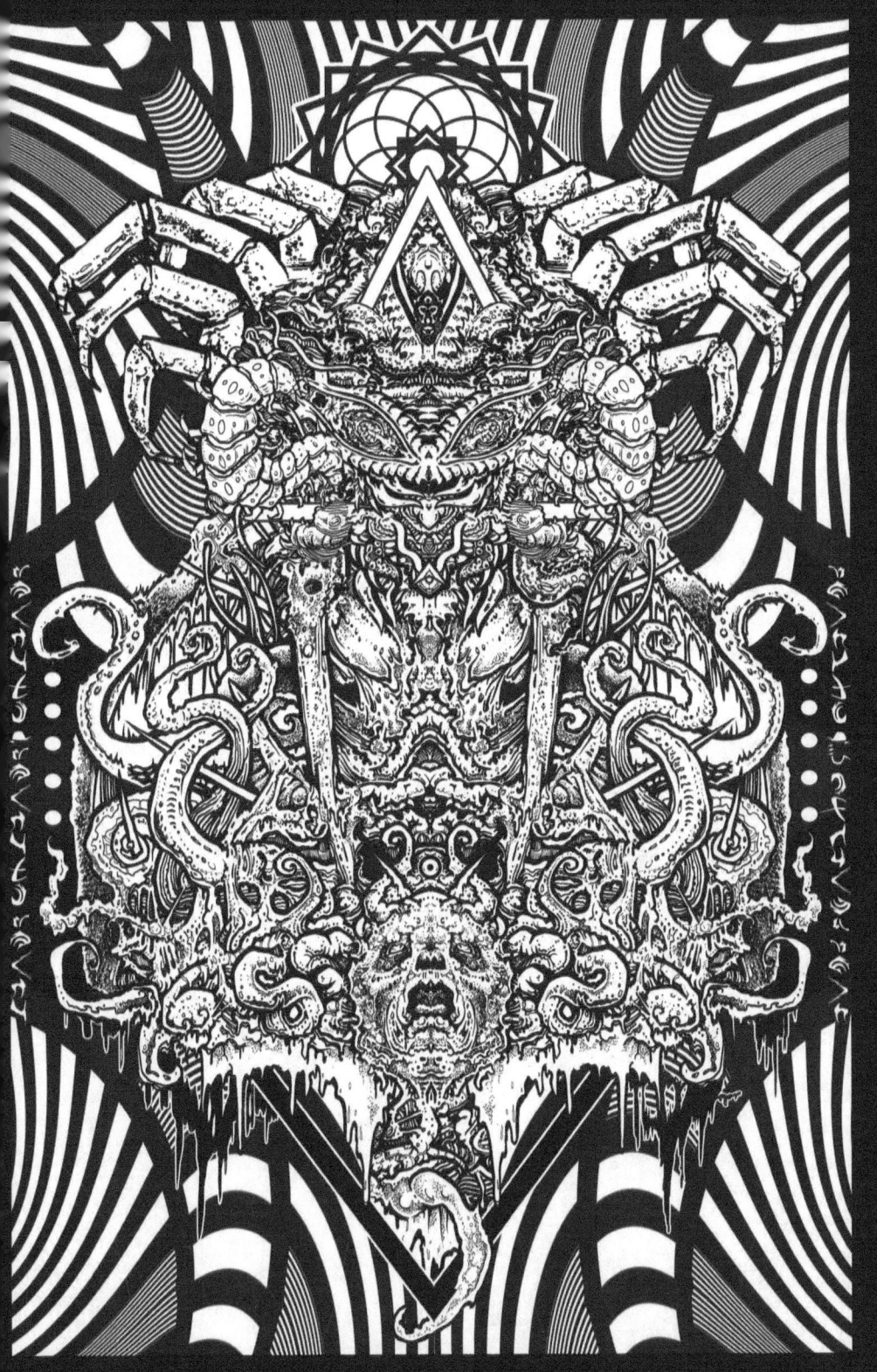

Dispensing of Parasitic Thoughts.

Shadow healing is a powerful and necessary tool in the utility belt of Sovereignty. Given the ability to extract unuseful thought patterns which inhibit unfoldment is crucial to those purifying the soul karma of even things from past lives to the daily attack of unstable psychic affairs of co-workers family and friends. There is a call to daily vigilance over our state o mind. The thoughts one entertains should be observed for sometimes they are not our own. If there are negative thoughts and belief patterns running in the background of the mind, than perhaps a beneficial exercise is the extraction or dissolution of these negative unserving aspects of thought.

The mind is a fertile field and we must consistently tend to the extraction of weeds. This is the archaeology of the internal landscape of the psyche. What is the origin of desire, for each vice is a slave driver that keeps a man under the whip of obligation to wants and needs which may only serve to inhibit growth. Deep exploration must be done to find the core of our base desires which lead to suffering. This is the awakening to our self defeating thought processes. This is growing up. The problem is not external, it is the elements of the inner world which projects itself on the outer world. The confused mind attracts more confusion. The mind perverted with thoughts of shadow will attract greater shadow. These belief systems must be extracted through shamanic work. This takes discipline. Discipline and hard work will al-ways prove to be your best friends who do bring gifts and rewards the likes of healing and upliftment. However we must first desist in putting off the initiation of these efforts and step right into the enactment of such methods as to look inward. It is not always a pretty state when we inwardly cast our gaze. There may indeed be some shadows to turn light upon. Extraction and processing of old beliefs and inhibiting patterns of thought are similar to the way you would pull a splinter from your eye. With intent to purify and do the work of extraction one can cleanse the inner landscape of these parasitic mind critters. They serve us with lessons, but those lessons can mostly be appreciated when the shadow work is done. Use the guidance of heart. Roll up the sleeves and delve deep into this healing practice is to come into great health, well being and advanced wisdom. Like a pond clogged with tree branches and debris, the waters of emotion will lead to a flood of purifica-tion where energy can flow. For it is the hand of man that is responsible for enacting the will of mind. Exert great discipline of what wills your hands choose to express. For what you put out will come back unto you three fold. So clean up your inner landscape of shadows and parasites and walk in the light of an upgraded system of ethics and high standing character. This is the great work .

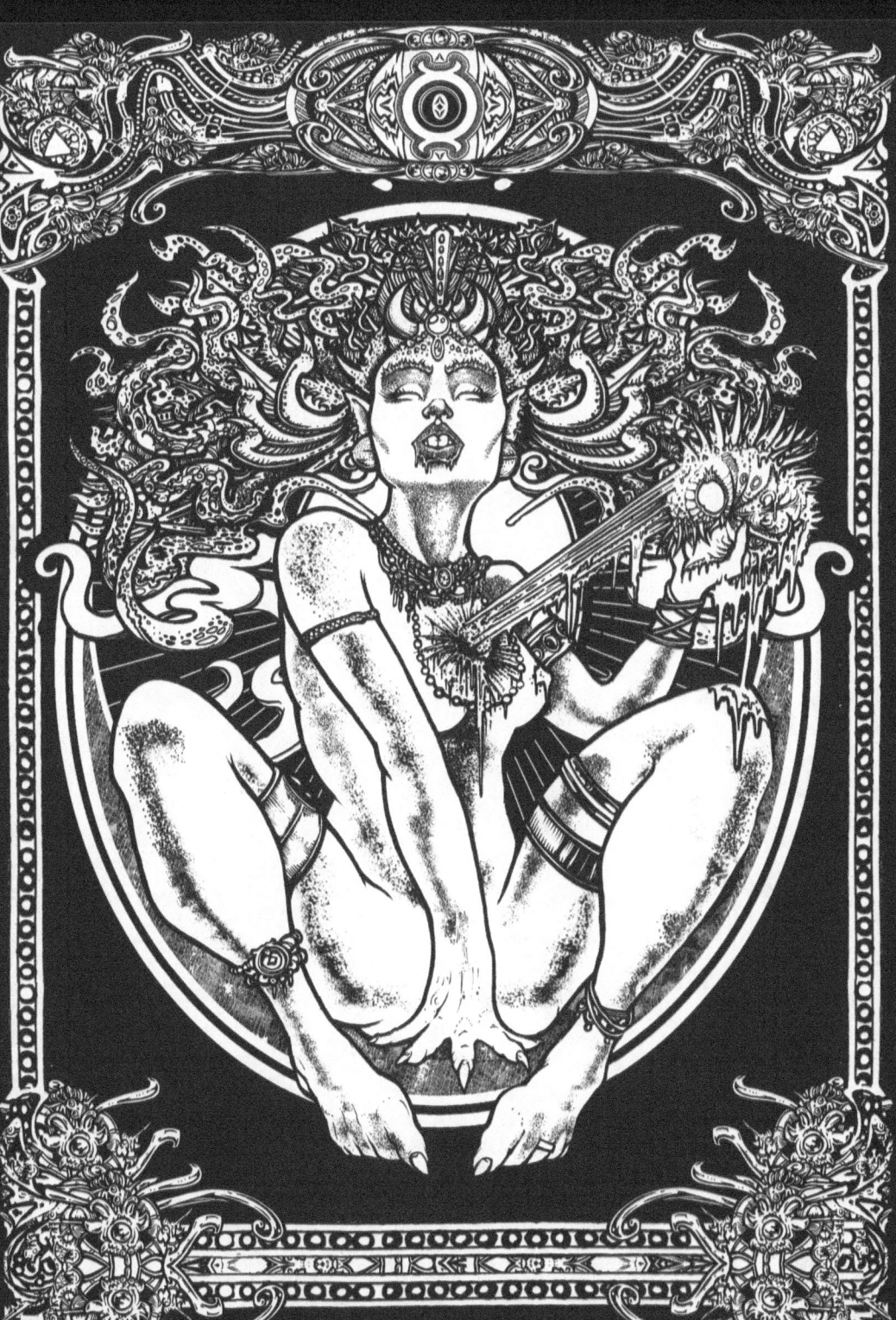

The Formless Death beyond the veil.

The only real death is the de-ressolution of the consciousness. Lifetime after lifetime that inner sense of awareness, that facet of the creation awakens within the individual. Though the body turns back into dust, consumed by Sophia becoming the fertilizer for new flowers to blossom. The true self goes on to understand more and more on its unique path home again and again and again. This is immortality, this is our truest form. This can be devoured and obliterated too though in the jaws of chapel perilous. For one path brings you back into the light, and the other, a self serving parasitic ridden path leads into the jaws of defragmented computer virus de-resolution vortex machine. It is in place to defragment the unamiable components of the reality simulation. Just as a super computer syphons outcomes that do not fit within its program paradigm so too will rogue negative consciousness be shifted out of reality at the end of the unfoldment cycle. The defragmented aspects will be cast into new creations in new universes born in new timelines far beyond our mental grasp.

 Is it your choice that your existence shall be scattered and cast as fertilizer to unborn stars? Or do you wish to maintain your sovereign sense of awareness and live eternal? For this is the one path of salvation, to climb the tree of knowledge and sit upon its lofty heights reclaiming the crowned glory.

For the fool tread with out fear just as the wildebeest goes to drink of the river. There the jaws of the crocodile eagerly awaits the consummation of the dead hearted.. So are the higher realms wrought with even more complex forms of danger which do seek to destroy and consume your mind out of body. Yes there is a fate worse than death, and that is eternal death, that is a severing of the stream of consciousness, that your quantum essence be devoured by larger hounds, fallen gods that care not for your personal freedom or universal destiny. Be aware, for those who tread outside of circles of protection face these black hole entities, the destroyers, the vampires of the cosmos. Dead light wishes to feed upon your soul. In this exercise of free will, which is our universe, there are many who have chosen to stray as far from creation as possible, testing the very boundaries of infinity. In such deviations the inner light weakens and dies. For the consciousness to maintain itself it must adapt to predatory devourment of other sources of living light, rather than to reestablish a connection of its own. Through negative emotions, fear and patterns of deprecating thought they sip upon the healing waters of the soul for as long as the well spring of godliness persists within such pityful of victims.

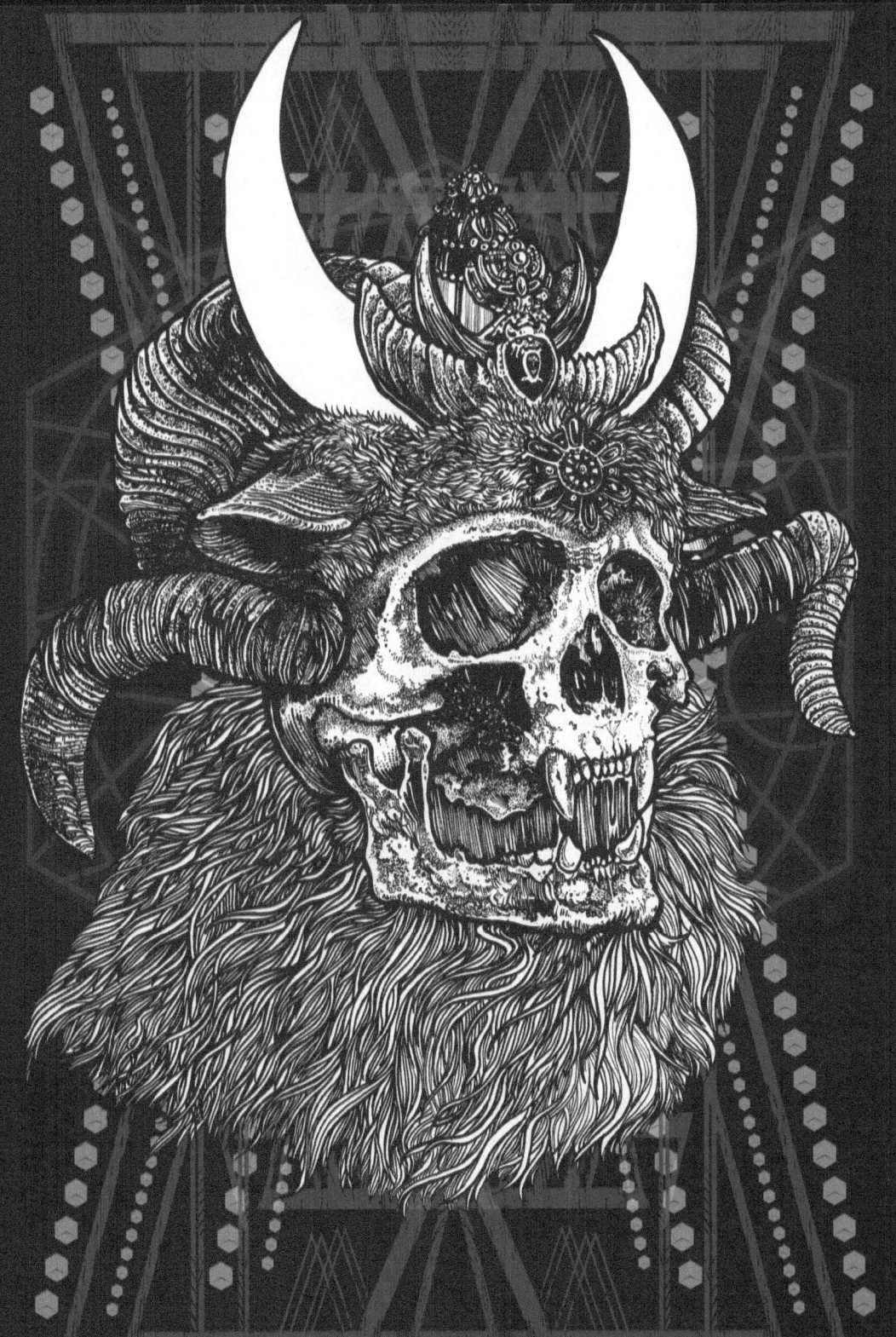

Soul Retrieval

This will take much inner work to observe and heal.

The contagion of spiritual putrescence can and should be removed from the aura in all timelines. When you silence your mind and still your body you can become aware of the energies surrounding you. While in the meditative state visualize yourself from outside of your self. See your meditating body as becoming as clear as possible. You may notice fuzzy or dark areas that refuse to bend to your vision. Something has fastened itself to your auric field that aught naught be. Mentally and physically pull off these darker colored areas. Imagine energetic saw blades of light emanating from your hands and physically cut any tentacles, tethers, ties or roots from you. Especially focus on your heart and solar plexus. This may release a great deal of emotion and trigger memories of harms done to you. There are actual pieces or fragments of your soul that have been "stuck" in that moment in time where the hurt literally fractured your being upon occurrence. These aspects of your fractured soul are lost and it is your shamanic duty to heal them and reunite those aspects in a healing and maternal way.

Look through your lifetime and you may see younger aspects of yourself which are still disassociated. You must reclaim these aspects. Call to them, understand that the pain was as real as it was illusionary, for we are in a matrix of learning, and this process of reintegration will be much like a virus search on your computer. Call out to all of your lost soul fragments to return to you in love for the purpose of full processing and integration. View outside of yourself all the aspects of yourself along the time span of your life. By offering gifts forgiveness and understanding from your new found perspective you can beacon the aspects of the fractured soul to come back to you, filling your human body and reintegrating with you in a most sacred and healing manner.   Soul retrieval is a vital Shamanic tool which will result in a fuller, happier resonance. The more of your soul that is actually in your body, the more you will resonate or sing with the spirit of creation, which is your most natural and original state.

This is healing work. This is the most sacred and unspoken of work. For even the finest china is never lost but a chip in its even most dramatic of falls from the cupboard. It is always brought back together again and sewn with the golden glue and considered better for the new aspect of character. This character is the adornment of experience that eternity anticipated by falling into materialization in the first place.

A practice of meditation and aligning the clear chakra points will result in physical vibration, auditory and visual hallucinations and heavy emotional release. A private and safe environment is recommended .

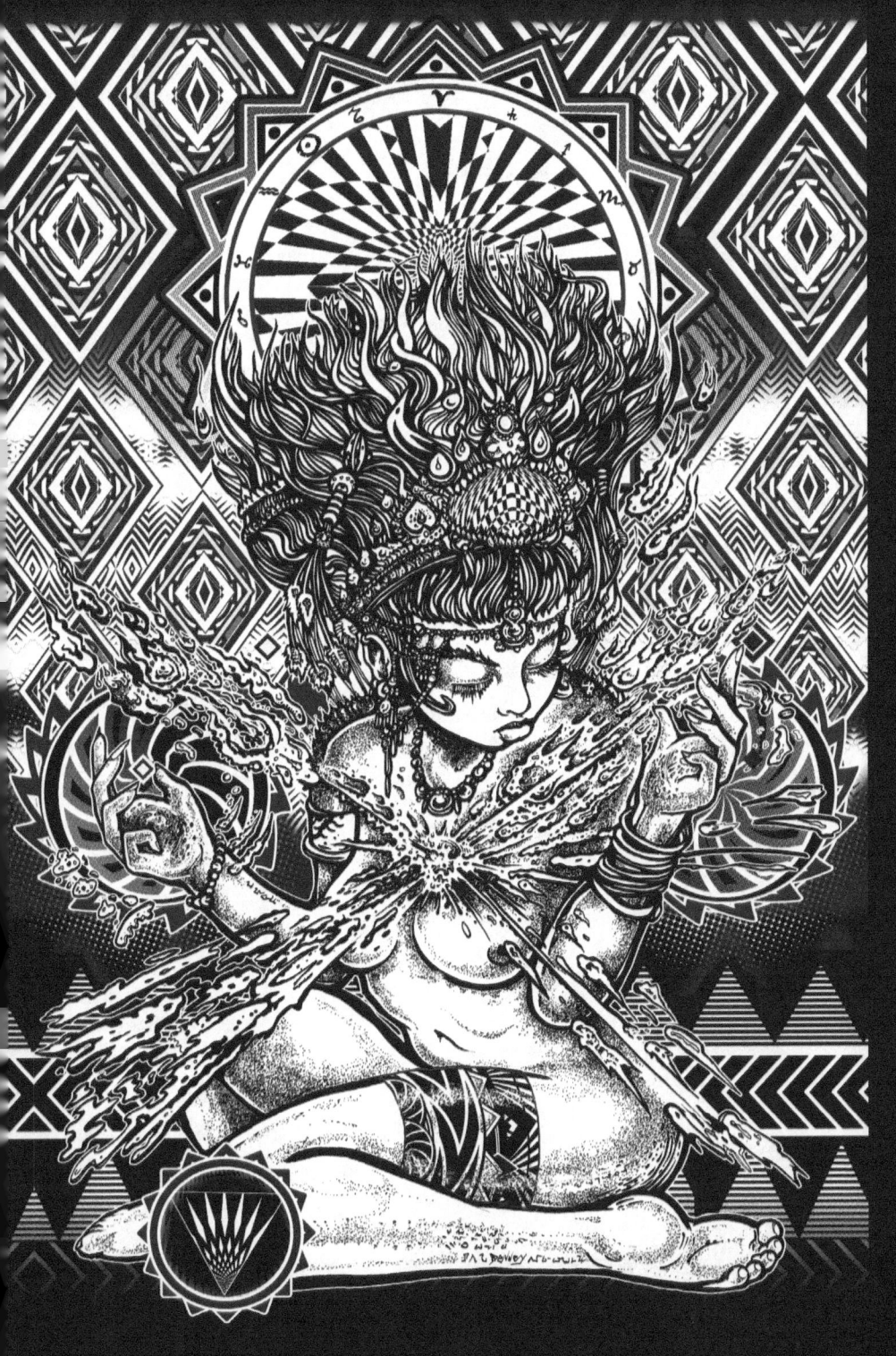

The Queen of Opportunity.
Take the leap of faith into the darkness of uncertainty for that is where Op
portunity awaits with great gifts. If only ye excerpt the confidence to accep
her will you find rewards. Breathe, breathe deep and slow for in your breath
is the power to generate great magic. In the breath is the understanding of
the organism of the universe. The simple yet fundamental act of convert-
ing molecules of oxygen into vital sustenance for the blood stream is in the
maintenance of solid deep breath. In the moment is where we find it, the
gifts of epiphany of the only one thing that is real enough to experience, the
hear and now.
This Queen of ancestral knowing comes to us in the dark night of ignorance. With an engaging gaze of some deep ephemeral knowing she points
to the strings which connect all things. The fragmented inner workings of
the heart crystal matrix glows as its tethers are agitated. The various angles
reflect and record the ephemeral and incubate the intent like a flower bud
set to blooming. Stars like diamonds glimmer even in the depths of moon
kissed twilights. So reign down from on High Saturn, cast those instruction
over the web and encode the seed deep within the subconscious of your
devotee. For all things are connected, and to the connection we can raise ou
selves through the ancient and free act of the breath. In deep, deeper than is
comfortable and then hold it there. In that silence is the whispering winds,
in that place is the void opening up speak. Rise to the coalescence with this
spirit field of knowing. For the soul is a web of information connected to ou
heads by such strands. You can feel it activating, like course waves of energies often accompanied by chiming tones and euphoria. This is the vortex
point activation, this is the act of connection to that field. A place where all
things are known, and where all experience is stored.
  We have left ourselves time capsules. These are artifacts of DNA information deep within our inner crystal matrix. These are the codes of accessing
these inner star gates. The stars rain these gems of access reverberating the
voice of heart. That which resonates with the original voice of the Creator,
that first thunderclap of expansion. This we will stumble upon in dreams, it
is the way by which we shall reconnect with our wings, our angelic heritage.
For the web of life run deeper than we are capable of perceiving at this time.
Through the breath we reconnect with our source field of knowing, the core
of wisdom and inspiration, thus we rise, we raise our vibrations. Pulling the
strings to achieve proper frequencies of reception. Once we remember our
wings free shall we fly ourselves from the trappings of the spiders web of
Kronos.

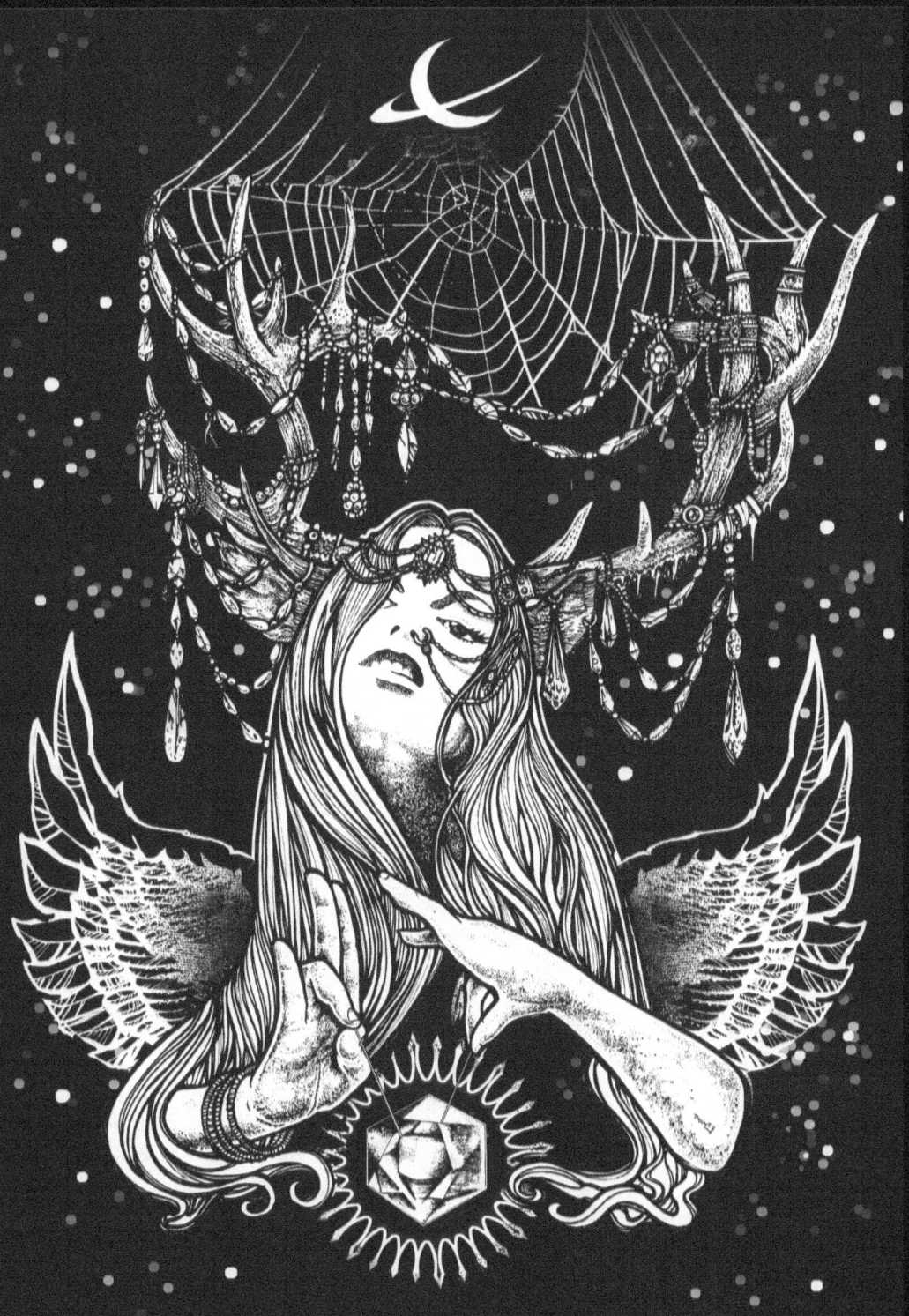

The Heart of the Earth.

The Goddess Sophia. For all things are alive and have a soul. She is the spirit of the Earth. She is our Mother in more ways than can be described in human language. Her own heart is the portal by which our souls did travel to be incarnated. She knows each and every one of us intimately down to the very code of DNA. She birthed us etheraclly first and then we came into conception. Such a deep rooted connection extends beyond lifetimes and reverberates multidimensionally as we dance through the cosmos in a symbiotic cycles of incarnation. She is our space ship, our ground, our maternal source. She cries out to our hearts and through our hearts we connect with her. Through dream and meditation to hear the voice of her we strive feeling the soul of the world. A living growing planetoid hurling through space in a dance that only the greatest of creators can bare witness. Sophia is in great peril now. She has a personal message for you as she reaches out amidst the chaos of cell phones and internet devices, multimedia advertising and brainwave altering wi-fi. The smog of her burning lungs clouds the minds of her children who forget and act as zombies, chopping away slowly piece by piece the body of the mother. Burning and stabbing and poisoning her as she screams out for her children to wake up!

Part of the duty of this day is to hear this voice of Sophia. The mission to silence the chaos and tune in with the heart to hear the subtle tones and reverberations inside. The listening to the cries of the Earth is the most overlooked aspect of the great work.

This connection is in part the activation process of personal individualized ascension access codes. This is the stirring of the DNA, the very receiver/transmitter of reality that was so intimately encoded when the soul went through the Sophia Matrix in order to incarnate on her. We all were literally birthed through her, and by returning to her in thought and heart, we reactivate our original encoding. The modern day bombardment of bogus malware and pernicious virus software all becomes entirely deactivated through the process of ascension access code activation. Connecting daily with Mother Sophia greatly expedites the level and manner in which these codes are reintegrated into our daily lives. The unfoldment then becomes exponential. Like a domino rally of light work. Each incarnate human passes their activation to another. Like a song, the DNA sings in harmony when these codes are initiated. Through the gift of the loving and life giving Sophia, we hear her voice, and download with it the message and the work she needs us to do. Every person plays a small roll and when unfoldment comes into effect, every little piece of the puzzle builds the bigger picture of healing and reclamation.

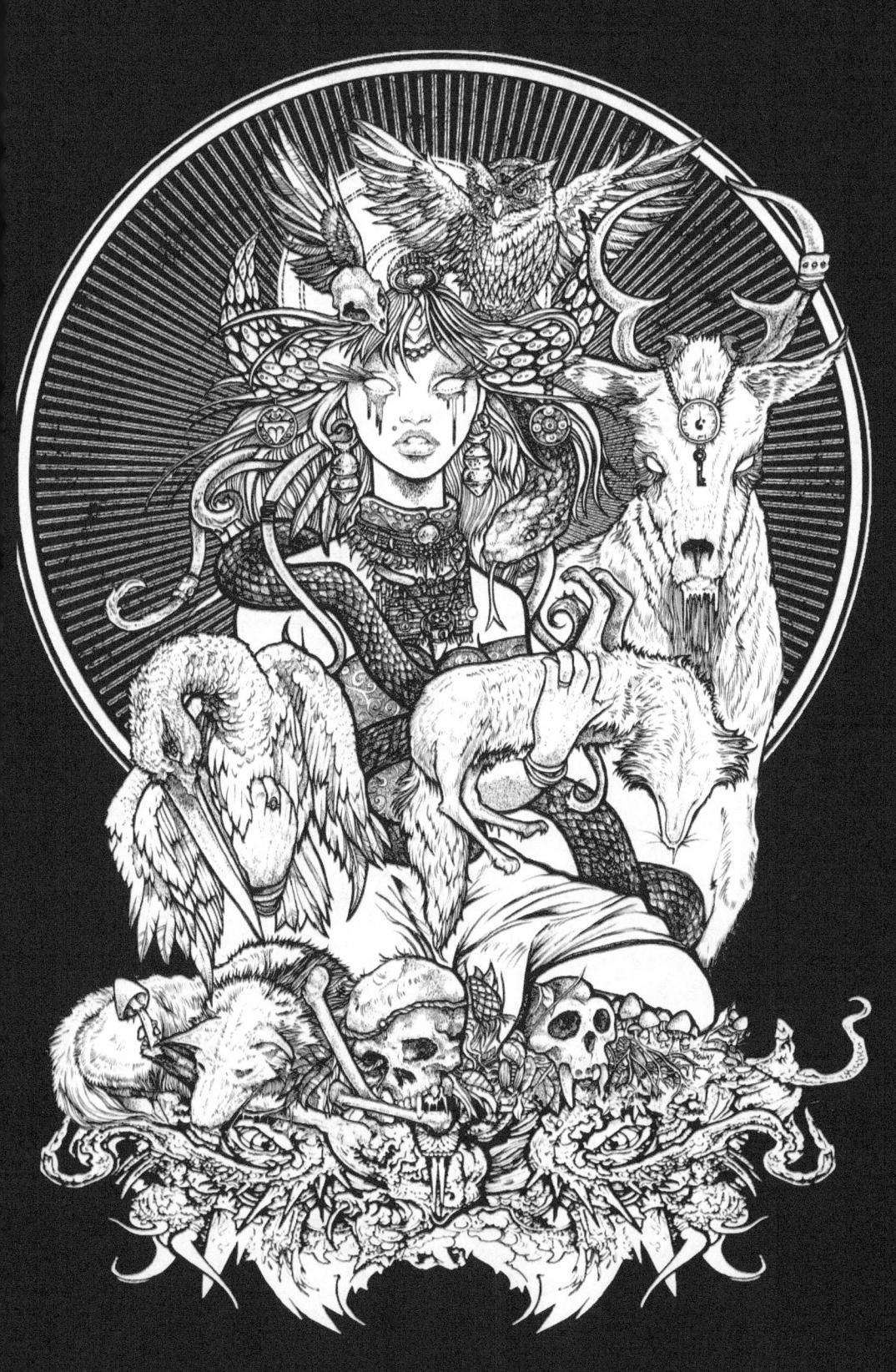

The Golden Angel.

Near the end our journey, at the highest point awaits us that dawning of the mind. The symbolic activation of the pineal gland, the unseen eye of inner light becomes as the watchtower guiding the tormented traveler through the oceans stormy wraths to lands of solace and safety. Awakened it opens to see upwards through the paradigm of thought built illusion, deeper through to the unfolding blossom of the multiversal alignment. The truest reflection of source back unto itself. This the end of the road of realization that consciousness is riding, that hexagonal particle of light tracing the edges of the mandala around a toroidal loop of conclusion and rebirth.

Here is where the trials of alchemical fire culminate in an illumined royal coronation at the cathedral the cosmos. The iniquities of the adept have been burned away by trial of fire as too the resistance been boiled away the impurities of lead. Cleansed now is the robe of aura which shines a bright heavenly white as we ascend the step towards the throne room. The platform is purified and the holy union is sanctimonious. Here is the attainment of the Father onto the Womb of the Mother, the fertile Queen of the Infinite. Where the spirit and mind of Man amalgamate in One sacred and unending moment stretching eternal through all aspects of timelessness. The dance of tone from two on top of every molecule of matter back into one is the serpents dance. Woven like a fabric of unfathomable love spiraling out through the void seeding yet again new and unimagined realms.

The ecstasy in the eyes is the sight of the end of the road achieved now. The bliss emanates from the knowing of the journey reflected back upon as fragments of timelessness collapse in on itself. The gaze is drawn to the center of the black hole that is the eye of allness. Found in every particle of light or a grain of sand can be seen this greatest handywork of the architect. That which did mold and intended to unfold. Each took the universe time to create, and in that creation lies the Source. The wisdom of the stars, and the extraordinary powers that lay embedded within their ancient processions becomes known, as their dance reveals the pattern we all must walk. Once the key has been found to open the door way to All, so Semjase will be there with you. The final blessing and reward of the great work. This knowledge is the bridge which we have built by way of self initiation from the heart of the Earth to the Soul of the Sun. This connection will make for a new being, a new Human, a divinely inspired Mankind. The old man will fall away like the shed skin of the grown serpent. Out of the stone it slithers towards the light with a fresh coat of iridescent amber scales disappearing into the mystical orb of golden horizon. Shining as a beacon of union is the new stuart of the kingdom, the pure warrior magi.

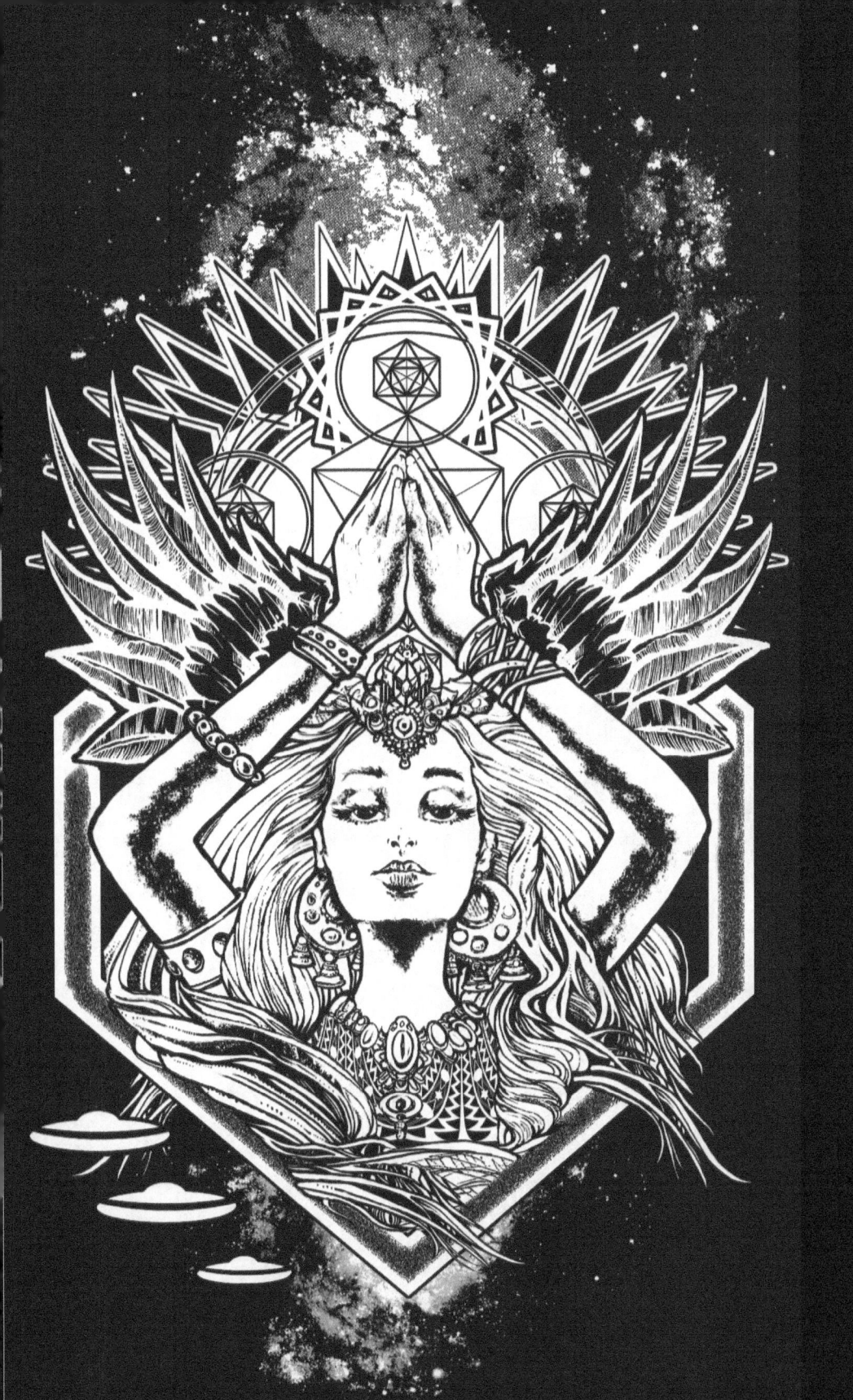

In summation

The dawning of the mind is the prescribed unfoldment process of the evolv
ing human as fractal fragment of the multiverse. I believe that it is the great
intention of the spirit that moves cosmos to connect with every creature and
intelligence that dwells within it. Perhaps you have a subconscious recogniti
of these symbols and words, which may be why you find them fascinating.
This is the law of attraction, one is attracted to the vibration of that which is
inherent to this personal dawning. Like the sun flower blooming to embrace
the rays of the rising dawn to ingratiate itself with such power. The great arc
tect embedded these geometries into every working cog of this reality. Hum
consciousness is much like the operating system of a computer. For instance
Windows computer from the 90s wouldn't have the software to do download
and decode a website from 2015. The java and flash encoding would be too
complex for it to decypher, and if you tried to use your computer from 1992
log into a modern website you would be presented with errors and blockage
The computer would not even recognize or be able to download the code. Th
practices and ideas prescribed here are allegories to upgrading a units ability
to Decode. Some people come in with updated software inherently, like a ne
computer they process information very quickly. Others must work towards
it. Either way due to some deep esoteric evolution, work done in other time
lines or lives translates and is activated from deep within. In ancient times
such a person would be called a genius. These are the artists, poets, scientists
shamans, musicians, those in touch with creation and practice their craft
daily. The moment you start playing with these geometries and incorporating
them into your own creations, you align to the creative force in all and auto-
matically upgrade your brain software. Also you become in tune, or begin to
sympathetically actuate to this vibration of subtle realities which heightens
intuition, awareness and triples creative vision. This is called by occultists, Th
Great Work. The building of the bridge between the corporeal trappings of
flesh to the etheric aspects of the spirit, the sense of the I AM. This is alchem
This is the courting of the higher self. There is MUCH which would not fit in
here. Yet with every act of creation incorporating these fundamental ideas th
artist pays homage to the Queen of the universe and evokes and integrates th
power of spirit, heart and mind. The resonance of these works will reach out
through time and inspire others who are on similar paths of awakening, ever
in those not yet born on this world. in these most prescient and heralded of
epochs the adept must engage the opportunity. The path calls through the ab
scess of space. The ability to recognize these symbols and resonate with them
validates and expedites personal evolution. We have an infinite destiny with
creation. The time of awareness is now. May the light be upon your breath an
the breath be onto your heart.

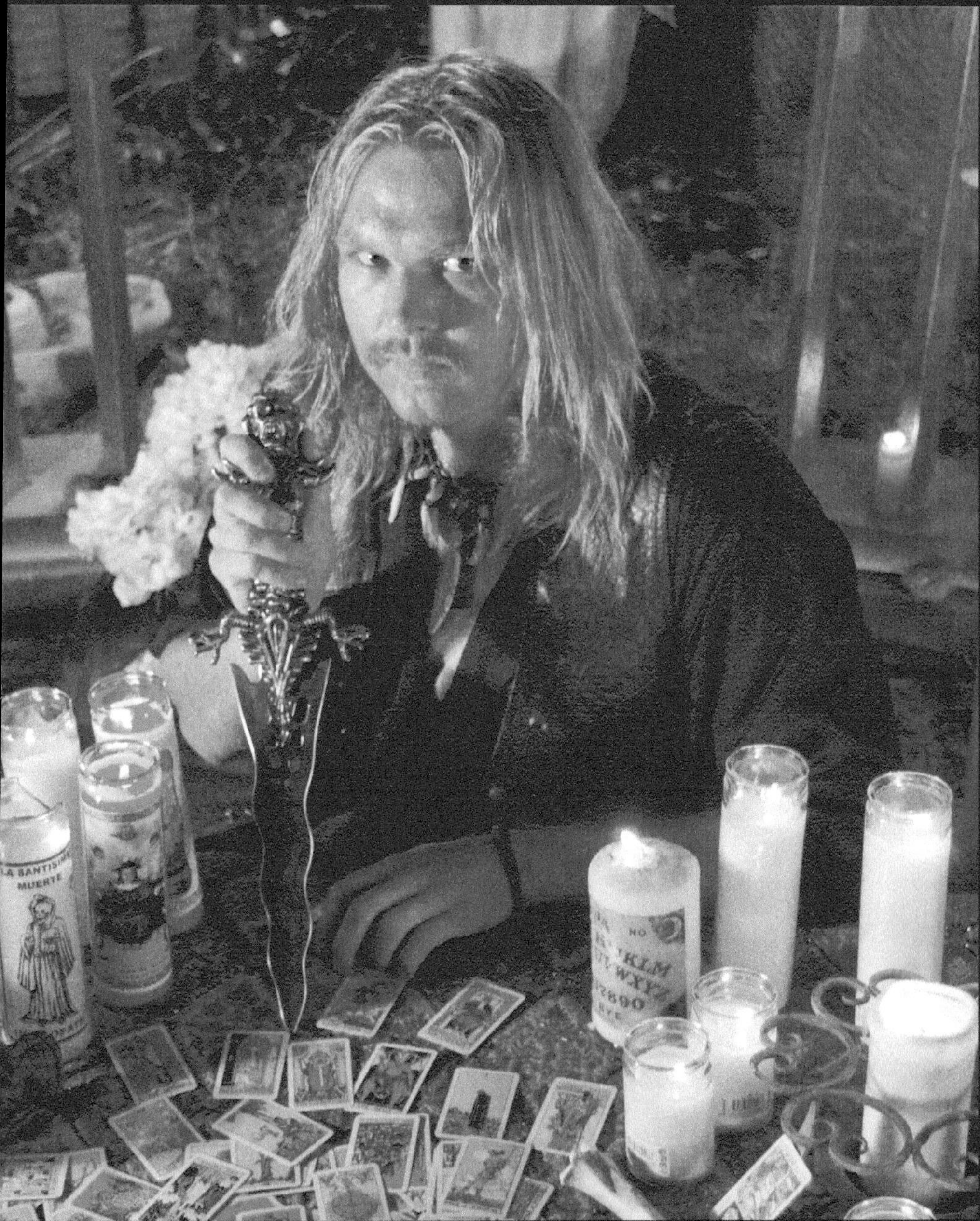

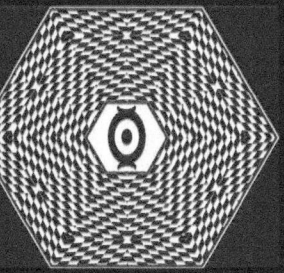

Dawning of the Mind
c2015 Tom Ambrose Denney
Written/Designed/Illustraited by Tom A. Denney
Printed by LuLu Enterprises Inc. Morrisville NC
Published by www.tomdenney.com
IsBN 978-1-312-05909-2